DVD INCLUDED

Dr. V's Pick

simply parenting

Understanding Your

W9-DDN-519

Newborn &

Infant

A multimedia guide for parents
on childcare and development
from newborn through
one year of age

Mary Ann LoFrumento, M.D., F.A.A.P.

This book is dedicated to the memory of Dr. Bayard Coggeshall,
who taught me the art of pediatrics and inspired me with
his practical wisdom and dedication to his patients.

and

To the memory of Dr. Samuel G. Oberlander
who dedicated his career to helping mothers and
who brought so many babies into this world.

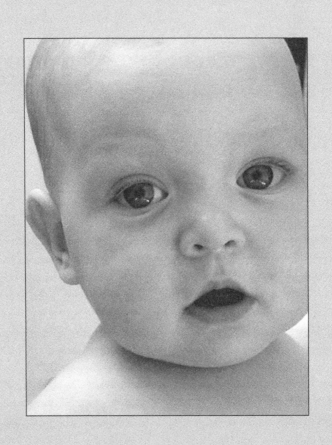

Acknowledgments I would like to thank all the nurses and pediatricians at Franklin Pediatrics in New Jersey for their editorial assistance, especially Dr. Fern Gotfried, Dr. Julie Ashton, Dr. Maureen Baxley, Dr. Marisa Rosania, Dr. Joan Sorenson, and Dr. Wendy Lee for their review of the material. I would like to especially thank Dr. Baxley for her contribution to the sections on feeding and nutrition.

I am indebted to Gerri Perkins, IBCLA and President of TLC-The Lactation Connection (Florham Park, New Jersey), for her editorial contribution to the section on breastfeeding. Her guidance and experience were invaluable in developing this section of the book. I am also grateful to Carolyn Varca for her help in updating the references and resource section and for her insights as a new mother.

I would like to thank my original editor Diane Dubrule for getting the book off the ground and my current editor Pamela J. Principe-Golgolab of PNA Associates Inc. for reorganizing and re-editing the book into its current form. Thank you also to Jen Conde at Franklyn Ideas for her work on the current layout. The creation of the DVDs would not have been possible without the hard work and expertise of my producer, Dawn Gual.

I am also grateful to all my friends, neighbors and family members as well as the physicians, employees and patients of Franklin Pediatrics and the staff and parents of the children at the Y's Owls Day Care Center of the Morris Center YMCA who allowed their babies to be photographed for this book.

And finally, I am grateful to my husband John for his long term support of this project and to my daughter Elizabeth for her valuable insight and advice.

By providing basic information on growth and development, nutrition and safety, we hope to give you the foundation on which you can build your knowledge through reading, lectures and other activities. This book and DVD is intended to compliment, not substitute for your pediatrician or family practitioner. Any time you have concerns about your baby's health or development, please consult these experts.

Mary Ann LoFrumento MD, F.A.A.P.

Born and raised in New York City, Dr. LoFrumento attended Barnard College and then the University of Pennsylvania where she received her medical degree. It was during her pediatric residency at Babies Hospital Columbia Presbyterian that she began writing simple outlines on childcare for parents. After moving to New Jersey, she started Franklin Pediatrics. For 17 years, she was the managing partner of this group, currently one of the largest pediatric groups in New Jersey caring for thousands of children. Immediately seeing a parents' need for accurate and easy to find information, she began expanding her outlines to include all aspects of childcare.

In 1996 she attended New York University and studied video production to pursue ways of enhancing her teaching materials. Shortly after that she founded HALO Productions and in 2002 Simply Parenting. Her unique approach to the production of multimedia products stems from more than two decades experience in clinical practice and medical education with a special interest in developmental and behavioral pediatrics.

Previously a Clinical Assistant Professor at Columbia University's College of Physicians and Surgeons, she is currently an attending physician at the Goryeb Children's Hospital of New Jersey and has remained active in teaching throughout the years. She conducts workshops for parents on all aspects of childcare.

She currently lives in New Jersey with her husband and daughter.

> "There is but one challenge greater than raising your child—trying to decipher all of the information that is out there."
>
> *—Mary Ann LoFrumento, M.D., F.A.A.P.*
> **Founder, Simply Parenting**

About Simply Parenting

When I opened my pediatric practice in 1985 and began seeing new parents and their babies, I was often asked for recommendations on books to read. As I worked to put a list together, I soon realized that there was a confusing amount of material that new parents would find on the bookstore shelves or in the handful of magazines devoted to babies and their care. In fact, as I began working with new parents, I realized that they were overwhelmed with information. Often times it was conflicting, coming from many sources including family members, books and the media. In addition, they were tired and under pressure with their new responsibilities and often did not have the time to read several books.

I decided to help them by putting together the essential information that they need to care for their new babies in an easy to read guide. The feedback was very favorable and patients constantly told me that these guidelines were all they needed for the basics.

Over the next 18 years, I revised and expanded *The Guide to Understanding Your Newborn* and provided my patients with the same easy to read guidelines on childcare from two months to five years of age. Whether a new baby came into a family through birth or adoption, just about everything a new parent needed to know was enclosed in these pages. Each provided brief descriptions of common concerns and problems. The recommendations were based on information from well-noted authorities like the American Academy of Pediatrics as well as insights from my two decades in private practice caring for thousands of patients.

Things are even more complicated for parents today. The bookstore shelves contain hundreds of books on childcare, there are several magazines dedicated to parenting and the "virtual bookshelf," the Internet, offers a seemingly endless stream of even more choices. Not only can you order books, videos and DVDs online, but also the Internet has provided new parents with access to hundreds of sites, each with their own version of important and useful information.

This incredible information overload can add greatly to the confusion experienced by parents and can leave them feeling quite bewildered and frustrated. And as childcare experts speak out on morning talk shows or the media points out one more thing that new parents have done "wrong," parents have lost confidence in their own judgment and abilities. They are frightened that they will harm their children if they do not listen to the "experts."

I feel new parents have plenty of confusion and what they need most is simplicity.

That is what *Simply Parenting* is all about. My goal is to "bring childcare back to the basics" and help you as a parent feel less anxious and more confident as you begin the most rewarding journey of your life.

Mary Ann LoFrumento, M.D., F.A.A.P.
Founder, Simply Parenting

How to Use This Book and DVD

This edition in the *Simply Parenting Childcare Series* contains two books: *Understanding Your Newborn* and *Understanding Your Infant* to help you through the newborn period and then the first year of life. Like all the books in the series, it is well organized and full of easy to find information. It contains just about everything that a parent needs to know during these years in a concise ready to use format. There are brief descriptions of common concerns and problems, combined with helpful, expert advice.

Throughout this book look for the "camera" icon. This indicates that this information is visually highlighted on the DVD, which is included in the back of this book. DVD chapters are linked to the age and developmental level of your baby. They provide a visual guide to normal development (The Two-Minute Baby), highlight safety points (Safe and Sound), and illustrate the best play activities for each age group (Simply Playing.) (Baby Care) reviews newborn bathing and skin care. (Breastfeeding Basics) illustrates breastfeeding positions and latch on technique. The DVDs are easy to navigate and designed so a parent can go directly to a specific section or watch the whole program.

As your baby grows, read or view each section a little before your child reaches that age. This way you will be prepared for your baby's developmental changes and how you need to adapt to them. When you have a question, search for the information using the book index or scan the topics in the DVD menu.

To further assist parents, at the end of each book I have also included a *Reference and Resources* Section with reviews of books, videos and web sites, which through my experience, I feel are good quality sources of information with the least amount of advertisements.

Our web site www.simplyparenting.com offers brief articles about common problems and normal development right at your fingertips. It also provides links to some other well-respected sites.

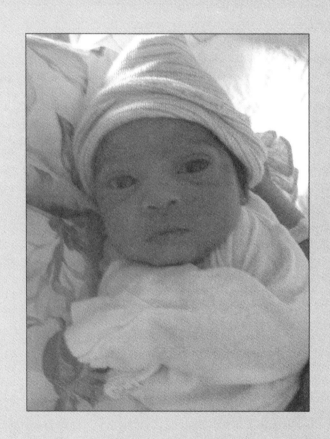

Your Newborn

Your Infant

General Information About Newborns and Infants

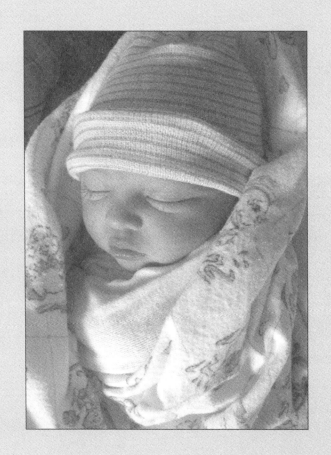

"Other things being equal, your baby will do well
if cared for with natural ease and given a goodly amount
of love…Friends and neighbors can often be of
great help, but each has his [her] own idea of
bringing up children and if you listen to all their advice,
you will be uncertain as to what is best for your new baby.
There is no single best way to care for all babies."

—The Baby Book, 1951
Prepared by the New York State Public Health Nurses

An Introduction to Understanding Your Newborn

This quote was taken from a booklet for new parents. It was the early 1950s. Formula feeding had been introduced to replace breastfeeding. There were fewer products on the market competing for a new parent's attention. And, Dr. Spock's groundbreaking book on childcare was the best-known reference for parents. Yet, these public health nurses knew babies well—from experience. Their approach was practical, down to earth and…simple.

Over the past 50 years, many "how to" books have been written that have "ruled the nursery" culminating in an explosion of advice offered in many different forms for new parents. Technology may have changed our lives in the 21st Century, but two things have remained the same: the emotions of new parents, and babies themselves.

As you take your infant home you will feel joy and excitement, but you may also experience feelings of anxiety and insecurity. This is perfectly normal and not surprising. Babies are rather simple. It helps to remember the following: New babies need to be fed, kept reasonably clean and loved a great deal. Do this, and your baby will be fine.

When you feel anxious and unsure, remember—all parents have nurturing instincts that guide them.

Use common sense and trust your instincts.

Enjoy your new baby!

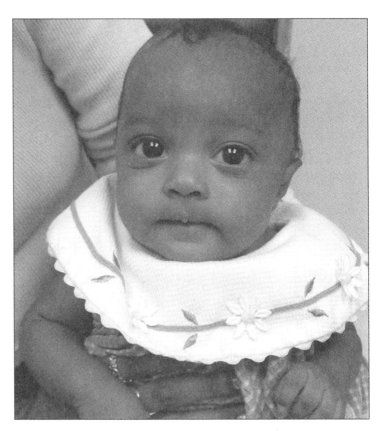

**Keep These
Points in Mind**

Your baby is an individual from the day he or she is born.

This includes differences in feeding, sleeping patterns, personality and temperament. This means that right from birth your baby is a unique little person. Therefore no one method can be applied to all babies. And what is right for one baby and family may not be right for another.

Family, friends and our culture will place tremendous pressure on you to conform.

If you decide to do something just because of these pressures, and not because you really feel comfortable, you are not doing yourself or your infant any good.

Advertising for infant care products is carefully aimed at your insecurities.

The message is that these products are essential to your child's health and well being. The reality is that you can do without 90% of these products. Be a good consumer. Carefully examine products and their claims before purchasing and read unbiased comparisons before making decisions.

Normal and loving stimulation is all that a baby requires for growth and development.

Smiling, laughing, and speaking to your baby will do just as much for his or her intellectual growth as all products designed to stimulate rapid development. A baby will not walk until he is able to walk, talk until she is able to talk, and will definitely not read at 12 months using flash cards.

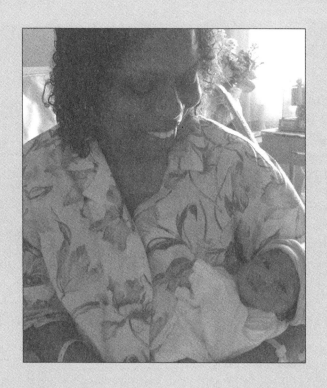

"Suddenly after nine months in the darkness and relative
quiet of the womb, they are plunged into a new world
of sights and sounds, movement, touch, tastes, and smells.
The ability to organize these sensations——to feel tranquil in
spite of them——is the first milestone."

–Dr. Stanley Greenspan
(Child Psychiatrist, Author)
First Feelings, 1985

Your Newborn in the Hospital

Appearance

The Head

During birth, the soft bones of the baby's skull are molded to allow the head to pass through the birth canal. This can produce an elongated head that will become more normal in appearance within one to two days after birth. The anterior fontanel, or "soft spot" can be found on the top of the skull where the bones meet. It is a tough membrane and will usually close over by 18 months of age. Soft swelling on the top of the head, known as "caput succedaneum" is not uncommon and can last a few days. Bleeding under the scalp during delivery can cause lumps known as "cephalohematomas." These may take weeks to resolve and disappear. None of these will affect the baby's brain.

The Face

Forceps Marks: If forceps were required during delivery, the face may be bruised. These bruises usually resolve within a week.
Vascular Marks: A blue vein often crosses a baby's nasal bridge. This will become less obvious as the baby grows.

5

"Stork bites:" So-called stork bites are pink areas found on the forehead, upper eyelids, and back of the neck. They are a collection of tiny blood vessels and usually disappear by a year of age. The neck mark will probably stay longer, only to become hidden by hair. This, too, will fade over time.

Rashes: Newborns frequently have small white dots called "milia" on the nose for several weeks. They can also have a variety of newborn rashes from pimples to red blotches. These all resolve within a few weeks and cause no harm.

Sucking Blisters: Blisters may form on the baby's upper lip from sucking. These require no treatment.

Epstein's Pearls: You may also notice small white cysts on the roof of the baby's mouth. These are called "Epstein's pearls" and are of no significance.

The Hands and Feet

The hands and feet may appear to be a blue color for weeks. This is due to immature circulation and does not mean that the baby is cold. The hands and feet may also be peeling. This does not cause the baby any discomfort and does not require treatment.

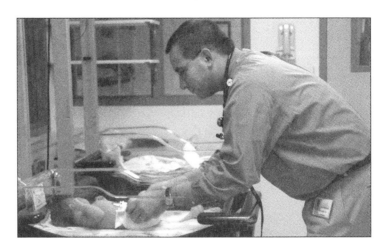

Procedures

Vitamin K Injection

Immediately after birth, your baby received a Vitamin K injection. This is done because a newborn's Vitamin K level may decrease at about two days of age. Since Vitamin K is important for the clotting of blood, the shot is automatically given to all infants to prevent bleeding.

Ophthalmic Antibiotic

Since the baby could acquire an eye infection (conjunctivitis) during the passage through the birth canal, an antibiotic ointment is automatically placed in the eyes of all newborns. Years ago severe eye infections caused erosion of the cornea and led to blindness. The application of this ointment may cause some irritation but will prevent infection.

Umbilical Antiseptic

A purple-colored antiseptic (triple dye) is coated on the baby's cord after birth. This helps to prevent infection and helps to dry up the cord faster. The clamp applied to the baby's cord in the delivery room is usually removed after 24 hours.

Metabolic Screening

Before leaving the hospital, a series of metabolic tests are performed on newborns. They are tests for hypothyroidism, galactosemia, phenylketonuria, and sickle cell hemoglobinopathy.* The value in doing the first three tests is that these diseases can be treated. Although these diseases are rare, if left untreated they can result in permanent brain damage. The fourth metabolic test screens for sickle cell disease, a red blood cell disorder. Since the test for phenylketonuria (PKU) is only valid when obtained at least 24 hours after the infant has begun feeding, the test may have to be

* Please note that all of these tests are required by law in some states, but not necessarily others. Your pediatrician or family practitioner will guide you on your state's specific requirements.

repeated if you are discharged within 24 hours of delivery.

These metabolic screening tests are done by pricking the baby's heel, obtaining a few drops of blood, and placing it on a special paper. The paper is then sent to your state's Department of Health for testing. Any positive or questionable result is reported back to your pediatrician or family practitioner and, if this occurs, they will immediately notify you as to how best to proceed.

Circumcision

The decision related to circumcision rests with the parents. Recent research has demonstrated a link regarding urinary tract infections in babies who are not circumcised. If you decide against circumcision, discuss this issue with your pediatrician or family practitioner. Unless a religious ceremony is planned, the procedure may be done before your baby leaves the hospital.

General Information

Breathing

You may notice the baby's breathing patterns are irregular, consisting of gasps, chokes and sneezes. Occasionally, he may even stop breathing for very brief moments (less than 20 seconds). These short pauses are perfectly normal.

Hiccups

All babies hiccup. The hiccups are not harmful and do not even appear to bother the baby. It may amuse them when life gets dull. They become less frequent by three months of age.

Moro (or "Startle") Reflex

A normal and frequent reflex in newborns (up to four months of age) is a symmetric opening and closing of the arms when the back is stroked or when the head and back touch a hard surface. Some babies do this quite frequently in the first weeks of life and may also react this way to loud noises.

Stools

While in the hospital, the baby's first stools are a dark green (almost black) color and they are very sticky. These stools are referred to as meconium stools and may be present for a couple of days. This first stool should be passed within the first 24 hours. The doctors and nurses will be checking for this. Thereafter the stools will change to a "transitional" or looser greenish-brown color. By the third or fourth day they become more typical: yellow and seedy.

Breast-fed babies may have "explosive" stools, which may occur as often as ten times per day. Bottle-fed babies tend to stool less and their stools are of a more formed consistency.

Stuffy Noses

All babies sneeze and seem to have a stuffy nose. Babies must breathe through their noses and because they are small, even mild congestion can sound noisy. This does not indicate a cold. Babies are never "born with a cold." Do not treat the baby for congestion with over-the-counter medications. In the winter months, a cool-air humidifier may help keep little nostrils from drying up. If you are worried, call your pediatrician or family practitioner for advice.

Weight Loss

During the first few days of life your baby will lose weight. Babies may lose as much as 10–15% of their birth weight, mostly in excess water. (In a typical seven pound baby this can amount to about 11–16 ounces.) By the end of the second week most babies have regained their birth weight. One of the reasons your pediatrician or family practitioner likes to see the baby in his/her office at two weeks of age is to assure that this has occurred.

Jaundice

Jaundice frequently occurs in the newborn. The baby's red blood cells break down to form a pigment called bilirubin (among other things). The bilirubin undergoes further changes in the liver until it is excreted in the stools. Most newborns have an immature liver; hence bilirubin tends to accumulate, especially in the skin, giving the baby a yellow color. This is particularly easy to see in the white part of the baby's eyes. As the baby's liver matures and as the baby feeds more, the bilirubin is handled more efficiently and excreted. In a full-term baby this maturation occurs about the third or fifth day of life. In a premature baby, it occurs about the seventh day of life. Most mild cases of jaundice will resolve by themselves.

This normal process may be intensified if there is an incompatibility between the mother and baby's blood type (especially if mom has O blood type and the baby has A or B blood type). In this case, there are more break-downs of red blood cells, resulting in even more bilirubin. For reasons that are not entirely understood, breast-fed babies frequently have more jaundice than bottle-fed babies, but this is rarely a reason to discontinue nursing.

A blood test may be necessary to measure the bilirubin level. Most babies with jaundice have a peak bilirubin of less than 15 on the third or fourth day of life. An infant with a level of 17 or higher on the test may need to be followed for another day or two to be certain that the level does not exceed 20, and is in fact decreasing. If the bilirubin level continues to rise, phototherapy may be indicated. Phototherapy breaks down the pigments in the skin so that they can be excreted in the stool. The therapy does not make the baby uncomfortable and causes no known long-term problems. Phototherapy can now be done in your own home if your insurance will cover the cost of this service.

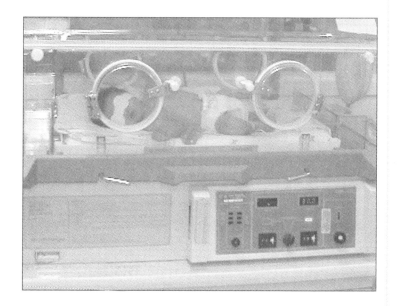

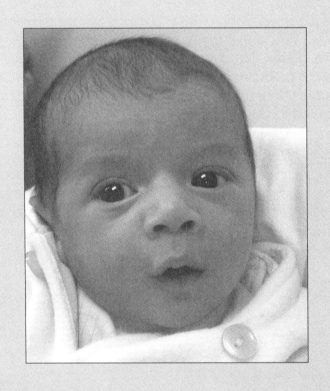

"There is no finer investment for any
community than putting milk into babies."

—Winston Churchill
(British Statesman)
Radio address 1943

Feeding Your Newborn

The choice of feeding method is a personal one and should reflect your own desires and life style and not outside pressures from friends, relatives or society.

**General
Information**

Normal Feeding Schedule

Whether you choose to breast-feed or bottle-feed your infant, mother/infant programs are designed to individualize feeding for each mother/infant pair. The nurse will help you find the right schedule for your infant. This is called *feeding on demand*.

Low Birth Weight

Babies who weigh less than six pounds at birth are considered low birth weight babies and will require more frequent feedings. Bottle-fed babies should be fed every three hours and breast-fed babies every two hours when possible. If you are breastfeeding a small baby it is not necessary to give extra water or formula over the first week until your milk is in. Water and supplements fill up the baby and make him less interested in breastfeeding. When the supplement is given with an artificial nipple it can contribute to nipple confusion. Breastfeeding at least eight to 12 times over 24 hours will help to bring in the milk quickly and help to avoid maternal engorgement.
If the baby is sleepy it is helpful to breastfeed when you see signs of light sleep such as arms or legs or lips moving or eyes moving under the eyelids.

Breastfeeding

If you plan on breastfeeding, please let your nurse know right away. This is a new experience for you and your newborn. If you have any questions regarding breastfeeding, please ask the lactation consultant or nurse while you are in the hospital or your family practitioner or pediatrician. Assistance is available should you need it.

Spitting Up

It is normal for some babies to spit up a small amount after feeding. The muscle between the esophagus and the stomach tends to be loose in newborns and consequently stomach contents come back up again. When the baby regurgitates, milk will simply roll out of his mouth. This is only a concern if the baby has progressive "projectile" (across the room) vomiting, if the vomit is bile-stained (green), or if the baby is not gaining weight.

Remember that the amount the baby vomits or spits up always looks like a lot more than it really is. During the first day of life, it is also normal for the baby to spit up a small amount of bloody mucous from the delivery. This problem usually resolves as the baby grows. If regurgitation is frequent, positioning the baby after feedings on his right side with the head elevated at a 30 degree angle may help.

Water

In very hot weather you may want to give plain water (but no more than about three to four ounces a day in between feedings.) Otherwise, *water is not necessary.* Even in hot weather water is not necessary for a breastfed baby and can contribute to newborn jaundice.

Signs of Dehydration:

- Listlessness

- Lethargy

- Skin losing its resiliency (when pinched, it stays pinched looking.)

- Weak cry

- Minimal urine output (one to two wet diapers is normal during the first two days, after that fewer than three wet diapers would be a danger sign.)

- Fever

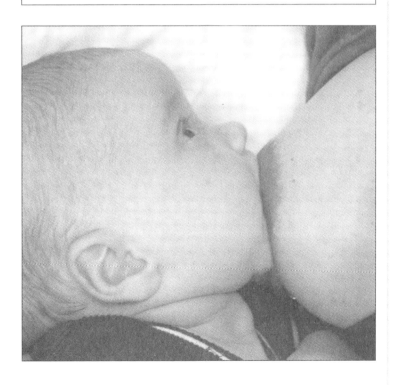

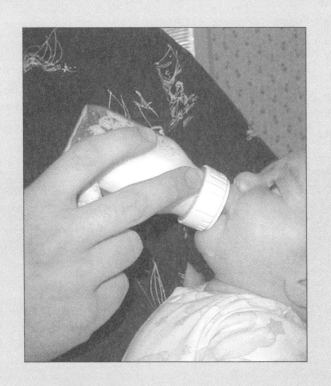

Bottle-Feeding

Frequency of Feedings

Most newborns will take three to four ounces every three to four hours. Some smaller babies will take less and larger babies will take more. In general, you can use the rule that the time between feedings will be approximately an hour per ounce of formula taken. (When I say every four hours, I mean from the start of the feeding.) Thus, if you start the feeding at 9 a.m. and the baby takes 40 minutes to feed, you would still count from 9 a.m. If the baby took four ounces, you would expect the baby to sleep until 1 p.m. Remember to burp the baby periodically throughout the feeding. If you cannot bring up a bubble, do not be alarmed—some babies swallow less air than others.

Types of Formula

There are two time-tested regular formula brands such as Similac and Enfamil with or without iron and some newer products such as Carnation Good Start, Similac Advance and Enfamil Lipil- (see DHA and ARA supplements below.) There are also soy-based formulas such as (Isomil and ProSobee) and hypoallergenic formulas such as Alimentum and Nutramigen. The soy and hypoallergenic formulas are used for babies who are sensitive or allergic to cow's milk. If you plan to bottle feed your baby and there is a family history of milk allergy, please inform your pediatrician or family practitioner as early as possible to discuss the options.

To prevent iron deficiency anemia, an iron-fortified formula is recommended right from birth. Many studies have shown that the iron in the formula will not cause constipation, colic or any other intestinal problem in your baby.

The formula in the hospital is in ready-to-serve three-ounce bottles. In the beginning, the baby may take only an ounce or so. This is to be expected until the baby "wakes up" at the fourth or fifth day of life. Usually, by the end of the first week, the baby will work up to taking between two and four ounces at each feeding.

Formula is available for purchase in stores in three basic preparations.

Ready-to-Feed: This is available in 32-ounce cans or in a six-pack of four-ounce bottles. Water must not be added or your baby will not get enough calories. This preparation is convenient but more expensive. The can may be kept opened in the refrigerator for up to 48 hours.

Concentrated Formula: This comes in 13-ounce cans and must be mixed with water before being fed to your baby. You mix it in a one-to-one (1:1) ratio with water (water and formula concentrate in equal proportions.)

Powdered Formula: This comes in a large can with a scoop inside. You mix it by adding one scoop of formula to every two ounces of water. This preparation is probably the most economical choice for occasional formula feedings.

Soy Formulas: Each of the major formula companies offers a soy formula preparation in which soy is the protein source (Isomil, ProSobee.) Soy formulas also differ from regular formulas in the type of sugar used as the carbohydrate component. Because the calcium in soy formulas can form a precipitate, even ready-to-feed bottles should be shaken well before being given to the baby.

DHA/ARA Supplements: Recently the major formula companies introduced formula containing DHA and ARA (two fatty acids that naturally occur in breast milk and that we consume in fish and meats). Claims were made that these fatty acids were essential to the developing brain and could "boost" a child's IQ and increase their visual function. Although some studies have suggested a small positive effect in the short term, others have not confirmed these benefits. There are no currently available studies that address whether any long-term beneficial effects exist. These formulas are more expensive and probably not essential to your baby's development.

Washing and Sterilizing

You do not need to sterilize bottles as long as you live in a town with sanitized water, you prepare only one bottle at a time, you wash the bottles in hot, soapy water using a bottle brush or in a dishwasher, and you refrigerate opened formula for no longer than 48 hours. You can prepare a full day's worth of bottles in advance (just keep the prepared bottles in the refrigerator.)

Storing Formula

If the baby does not finish all of a bottle you can leave it out at room temperature and offer it again up to one hour later. If you put it back in the refrigerator promptly you can keep it for approximately four hours.

You should warm a refrigerated bottle before offering it to your baby. This is usually done by placing the bottle under hot tap water, using a bottle warmer, or putting it in a pan of water on the stove for two to three minutes. The formula should be warm, not hot. Some people use a microwave to warm their baby's bottle. The danger here is that the milk can be heated unevenly with portions of it scalding hot and other portions cold. Consequently, the baby's mouth could get badly burned.

Feeding Position
Avoid bottle propping or feeding the baby in the lying down position. Milk gets into the eustachian tubes in the ears and can make your little one prone to ear infections. Feed your baby in a more upright position.

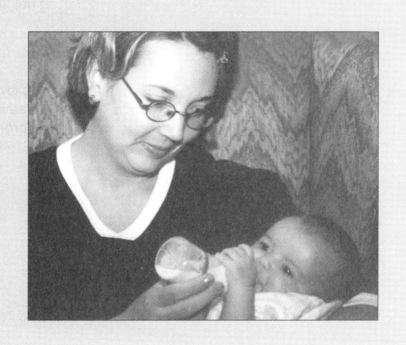

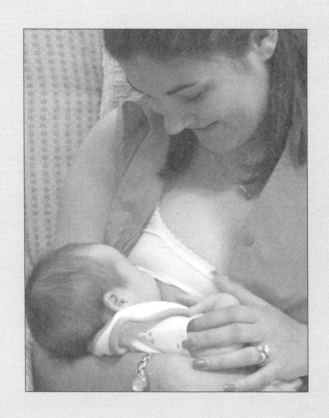

"The newborn baby has only three demands.

They are warmth in the arms of its mother,

food from her breasts and the security

in the knowledge of her presence.

Breastfeeding satisfies all three."

–Dr. Grantly Dick-Read
(Father of the Modern Natural Birth Movement, Author)
Childbirth Without Fear, 1979

Breastfeeding

General Information

Breastfeeding is natural, inexpensive and nutritious. It can be a wonderful nurturing experience for you and your baby.

Many mothers worry that if breastfeeding is not established in the first two days, the baby will be endangered. This tension may inhibit the letdown reflex and further delay your breastfeeding effort.

The normal, full-term infant is born with a protective "extra" amount of water. This protects the baby from dehydration while the mother is producing the early milk called colostrum and until the mature milk comes in on the third or fourth day. It also protects the baby for several days should a separation of mother and infant occur. This is how newborn infants have survived for up to a week during catastrophic events such as earthquakes. This should reassure the breastfeeding mother that the baby will not starve or dehydrate during the first few days of life before adequate breastfeeding is established.

Colostrum

The first milk called colostrum provides fluid, protein and sugars. It differs from mature milk mostly in the amount of fat it contains. Colostrum also contains many of the immune system factors, which help keep the baby healthy, as does mature milk. Colostrum is measured in teaspoons, not ounces, which gives the baby lots of practice nursing before the larger volume of mature milk comes in. It is normal for the baby to want to nurse long and often in the early days. Many babies want to nurse almost continuously for several hours and then sleep for several hours. Others want to nurse for ten minutes every 30–40 minutes round the clock. Newborns tend to be most wakeful between 9 p.m. and 3 a.m. and sleepiest during the day. When the baby goes through a painful procedure (heel stick, circumcision, injection, etc.) he may be unreceptive to breastfeeding until he is feeling better.

Labor and Delivery

Labor, anesthesia and pain medication can affect how sleepy the baby is as well as how able the baby is to suck in the early days. In the ideal delivery, mother and baby should bond before any hospital procedures are done—this includes routine cleaning and procedures by the nursing staff. However, this may not always be possible if there are any medical problems with the baby after birth or complications with the delivery for the mother. Since separation of mother and baby before the first feeding may result in feeding problems when the baby is returned, support of the nursing staff or a lactation consultant may be necessary to help establish a good breastfeeding relationship.

Frequency of Feedings

We recommend that you put the baby on a "demand" feeding schedule. This means that you aim to feed the baby when he or she is hungry. Many mothers report breastfeeding every two to three hours in the first two to three weeks of life or more frequently. If the baby will stretch out feedings for four or five hours during the night, that is fine. However, until the two-week well-baby visit verifies good weight gain, I recommend not more than four hours between feedings for babies weighing seven pounds or less.

Length of Feedings

How long should the baby nurse on each breast? This is quite variable. Babies usually nurse for 20–30 minutes on each side. Some babies nurse longer, some shorter periods. The same baby may nurse for different amounts of time at different feedings. Allowing the baby to determine when he is finished will ensure that he gets the right combination of the low fat fore milk and the fat-rich hind milk. Let the baby come off the breast on his own, then change his diaper to wake him and offer the other side. Often a newborn doesn't need to nurse the second side. He will let you know by clamping his mouth shut.

Is the Baby Getting Enough?

A good rule of thumb is this: if the baby is urinating well (six to eight wet cloth diapers or five to six disposable a day, by the third or fourth day (when your milk should be in), then he is getting enough. Another good indicator is the bowel movements. The baby should have at least three to four bowel movements a day (although this can vary) the size of a quarter after day three or four. If not, please call your pediatrician or family practitioner.

During the first few days there is no need for extra water or formula supplementation.

Breastfeeding Technique

Watch for early mouthing cues and immediately put the baby to breast. These include: baby turning his head to one side and opening his mouth wide, and putting his hand or fingers to his mouth. Crying in a newborn is often a late sign of hunger, so it is better to begin breastfeeding before a baby begins to cry.

DVD Chap 4

Latching on to the Breast

The goal is an asymmetric latch with the chin touching the breast first so that the lower jaw, which does all of the work, has more of the areola (the darker area behind the nipple where the milk is stored) compressed than the upper jaw. The baby's head needs to be tilted slightly back with his chin pressed gently into the breast and his nose away from the breast. Begin with the baby's "nose to nipple:" wait for a wide-open mouth like when the baby yawns, and then bring the baby to the breast chin first. Gently guide the nipple into the mouth.

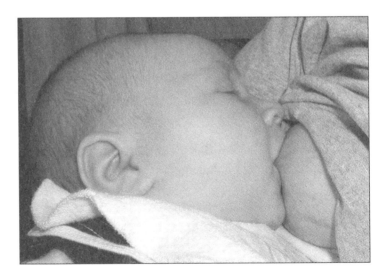

DVD Chap 4

Position

Since the mother will be nursing for several hours a day it is important to find a comfortable chair, sofa or bed in which to nurse. Use of pillows, bolsters, rolled up blankets or any other props to support the mother's arm or the baby's weight will help the mother relax. Even a small baby can feel heavy if the mother's arms are not supported. A stool helps some mothers to keep their feet flat on the floor and knees slightly raised. During the early weeks a straight back chair may be better for many mothers so they don't have to lean forward over the baby or lean back too far. Experiment to find the most comfortable position.

How to hold the baby to nurse: Bring the baby in close to the breast so that his face is right in front of the breast. The baby's head should be straight in line with his body so he doesn't have to turn his head to breastfeed. His ear, shoulder and hip should be in alignment.

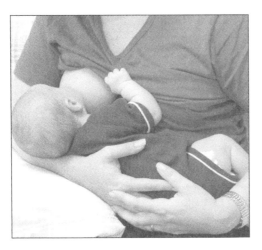

Cradle Hold

This is the most commonly used position. To feed on the right breast the mother holds the baby along her right forearm, supporting his back and allowing his head to fall back slightly causing the chin to touch the breast first in an asymmetric latch (see photo.) Pillows support the mother's back, arm and the baby if necessary.

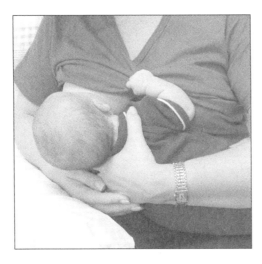

Cross-Cradle Hold

To feed on the right side the mother's left palm is placed on the baby's upper back with her thumb behind one ear and her index finger behind the other ear, her other fingers support the neck. This allows the baby's head to tilt back. This hold is good for the mother having trouble with positioning because she can see the baby's latch better. Again, pillows support the mother.

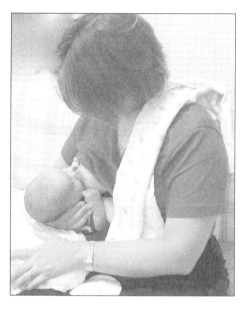

Football Hold

For the football hold the mother needs more pillows at her back so there is room for the baby's legs to be behind her. The baby's head faces the breast with his body tucked under the mother's arm at her side. The baby's bottom rests on a pillow near his mother's elbow. A common mistake is for the mother to place the baby too far forward so that the baby has to bend his neck forward to latch on or the mother has to bend forward, which gets uncomfortable. This hold is good for large breasted women and for small babies who tend to curl up at feeding time. For women who deliver by Caesarian section, it protects the abdominal incision from being kicked.

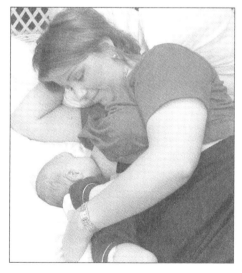

Lying Down to Nurse

Mother lies on her side with pillows under the head and between the legs. A pillow in the small of the back helps the mother not roll too far forward. The mother needs to place the baby on his side with his legs pulled in close to her. A rolled up diaper or receiving blanket placed behind the baby's back helps keep him in place. Some mothers need to raise themselves up on one elbow to latch and then ease them down into a more comfortable position.

Other Helpful Tips

Many women experience a "let-down" reflex as the milk begins to flow. This usually feels like "pins and needles" or a "tightening" sensation in both breasts. Other women do not seem to notice these sensations even though their milk is flowing well.

Never just pull your nipple from the baby's mouth or you may hurt yourself. To get the nipple out, break the suction by gently sliding your finger in the baby's mouth.

After the baby has stopped nursing on the first breast, offer the other breast. Do not be upset if your little one is just too sleepy to feed at both breasts. You may try gentle prodding. You may even wish to change the diaper or to burp the baby between breasts to help wake him up, but do not become frustrated.

Do not be surprised if you cannot get the baby to bring up a bubble. Breast-fed babies tend to swallow less air than bottle-fed babies and, in some, you may rarely bring up a bubble.

When you begin to nurse the baby at the next feeding it is a good idea to start with the breast you left off with. For example, if the baby nursed first on the right breast then left breast, at the next feeding offer the left breast first. This will assure that both breasts are stimulated to produce milk. Some women put a safety pin on their bra strap to remind themselves which breast to offer next.

In the first few days while nursing, you may experience cramps like menstrual cramps. This represents muscle contractions of the uterus and is completely normal.

Usually by about the third to fifth day your breasts will stop producing the early milk (colostrum) and begin producing the mature milk. At this time the breasts may feel engorged. They may feel large and tender. This engorgement only lasts a few days and then disappears. It is partly inflammation, which responds well to ice and an anti-inflammatory (like ibuprofen.) Occasionally the engorgement may interfere with nursing because the baby finds it difficult to grasp the nipple. If this occurs, before you put the baby to the breast you can pump some milk out, either manually or by using a pump (hand-held, battery or electric) in order to soften the breast enough for the baby to be able to latch on to the breast.

The use of a breast shield should be avoided unless advised by a lactation consultant.

Sore Nipples
The most common reason for sore nipples is poor positioning. Get help if there is pain. Even one incorrect latch can damage the nipple. Do not use soap or astringents on the nipples, even when showering. A daily shower or washing with water is sufficient. Apply a small amount of a lotion such as "Lansinoh for Breastfeeding Mothers" to the nipples religiously after every feeding. It must be kept on in order to do its job of healing the nipples.

It is important to remember that breastfeeding is not *purely instinctive*. It takes *learning* for both mother and baby. Do not feel defeated and give up. *It takes time and patience*. It is also important not to get hooked on a "clock and schedule" routine. Every baby has his or her own individual schedule.

Signs Help is Needed:

- Mother is experiencing pain during the feeding.

- Damage to the nipples.

- Breasts are engorged.

- Prolonged feedings (regularly more than 30–40 minutes on each breast.)

- Very infrequent feedings (less than three in first 24 hours.)

- Baby is not coming off the breast spontaneously.

- Baby is restless at the breast.

- Baby seems not satisfied after the feeding.

- Decrease in wet diapers (less than three in 24 hours.)

- The stools on the third day are still the green, sticky meconium stool that usually occurs right after birth or during the first day.

If you have further questions or need some help with breastfeeding, please call your pediatrician or family practitioner and he/she will put you in contact with a lactation consultant.

Breast Care

It is a good idea to buy a nursing bra with wide, non-elastic straps to provide good support. You may use disposable pads or cloth pads to absorb leakage. If you are more comfortable without a bra and leaking is not a problem you may go braless with no problems.

Mastitis

If mastitis (a breast infection) develops, nursing should be continued in order to keep the breast well emptied. Mastitis presents as a localized, hard, red, sore area in one of the breasts. You may feel like you have the flu. Apply continuous heat to the affected area, nurse frequently on the affected side and GO TO BED. Take the baby with you if you do not have help. If there is not a significant improvement in 24 hours, call your family practitioner or obstetrician who will probably prescribe an antibiotic. Although many drugs are secreted in the breast milk, most are not a problem for the baby.

Mother's Diet

You should maintain your health and continue the good eating habits you practiced while pregnant. Now is not the time to follow a weight-loss diet. You should continue taking your prenatal vitamins. Try to eat a variety of foods in as natural a form as possible.

Some women have found caffeine to be particularly upsetting to their newborn. It has also been noted that excess ingestion of cow's milk and eggs by nursing mothers may be associated with colic in their infants. Other foods (such as broccoli, cauliflower, cabbage, and chocolate) that seem to cause trouble vary from one mother/baby partnership to the next. If, after one or two trials, you notice that a particular food appears to upset your baby, try to avoid eating that food. *Unless you make a specific observation, it is unnecessary to restrict your intake of different foods just because you are nursing.* Alcohol may be taken in moderation.

You should drink enough fluid each day to satisfy your natural thirst (eight 8-ounce glasses of water a day). You might try working out a system whereby whenever you sit down to nurse the baby you drink a six or eight ounce beverage. You may drink water, juice or milk. You do not need to drink milk to make milk, but you do need to ingest sufficient calcium—1,200 mg per day—to preserve your own bone strength. But this does not have to come from milk.

Rest
Fatigue and stress can decrease your milk production, so be sure to get as much rest and relaxation as possible. Try to take naps during the day while the baby is sleeping. *My best advice for you is to over rest and follow your instincts.*

Bottle-Feeding Your Breast-Fed Baby

If you plan to eventually make a transition to bottle-feeding, or if you plan on doing a combination of breast- and bottle-feeding, I recommend that you introduce a bottle after the sixth week of breastfeeding. Waiting helps to avoid nipple confusion. If you must introduce a bottle sooner, wait at least until after the fourth week to allow breastfeeding to be well established.

The sucking motion on the breast and the bottle are different and some babies have trouble with the transition from one to the other. To make the transition a little easier I recommend the Avent (or similar) nipples. This nipple is longer, like a mother's nipple in a baby's mouth. Make sure you get the whole large bulb at the base of the nipple into the baby's mouth so his mouth is open wide like on the breast.

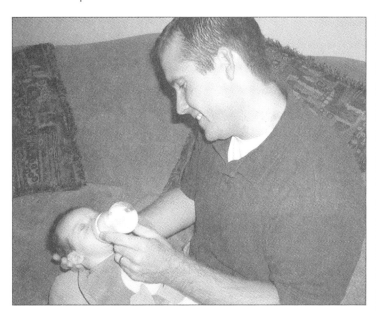

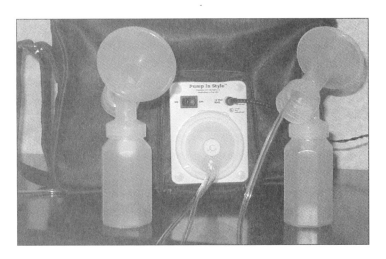

Pumping

You may use a breast pump to obtain breast milk for the bottle-feeding. These pumps can usually be rented or bought from the hospital or from lactation consultants in your area. If you are pumping to supply milk while you are away from your baby on a regular basis, you may want to buy a double electric pump like the one pictured here. You will obtain more milk by pumping both breasts simultaneously rather than sequentially.

Make sure you read all instructions with your breast pump. Keep your hands clean as well as all the parts of the pump that come in contact with skin or breast milk.

Make sure you are comfortable and relaxed. This is necessary for you to get a "let-down," which will allow the milk to flow. Listen to relaxing music or think of your baby (a picture can be very helpful.)

Pump no more than 20 minutes at a time.

The best time to pump will depend on individual factors. You will have the greatest amount of milk in the morning upon waking. Any time your baby has a bottle is a time you can pump as well.

Remember that the baby is a more efficient "pump" than any mechanical variety—how ever much you pump, the baby probably receives more from nursing directly.

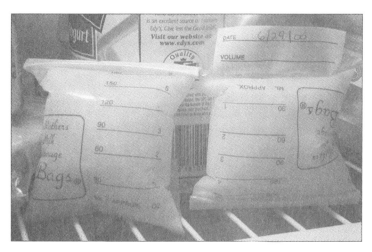

Storing Milk

The Rule of EIGHT: freshly expressed breast milk can be kept at room temperature (66° to 72° F) eight hours, or in the refrigerator for up to eight days. In a deep freezer, the milk can be stored for eight months (four months in a separate door refrigerator freezer).

Alternate "Milk Storage"—If you want to be more exact:

Term Colostrum (milk expressed within six days of delivery)
• At 80.6° to 89.6° F–12 hours

Mature Milk
At room temperature
• at 60° F–24 hours
• at 66° to 72° F–10 hours
• at 79° F–four to six hours
• at 86° to 100° F–four hours

In a refrigerator
• at 32° F–8 days

In a freezer

- In a freezer compartment located inside a refrigerator–two weeks
- In a self contained freezer unit of a refrigerator–three to four months
- In a separate deep freeze at a constant 0° F–six months or longer

The preferred choice of storage container for freezing milk is glass because it is the least porous. The second choice is clear, hard plastic and the third choice is cloudy, hard plastic. For maximum protection the storage container should be sealed with a solid, single piece lid. Some mothers choose to use milk storage bags specifically designed for freezing and storing human milk. If you use plastic bottle liners, use double bags to avoid tearing. (Fill any container you use only 2/3 of the way full because the milk expands when frozen.) Squeeze out the air at the top and roll down the bag to one inch above the milk before you close and seal the bag with a twist-tie. You may add fresh breast milk to already frozen milk provided you cool the fresh milk in the refrigerator first. Label the milk with the date it was expressed so that the older milk can be used first. If using in a day care setting put the child's name on the bags. Thaw breast milk in warm water.

Never microwave breast milk as it can burn the baby's mouth as well as destroy essential nutrients.

Previously frozen breast milk that has been thawed in the refrigerator or under running water should never be refrozen. It can be kept in the refrigerator for 24 hours or at room temperature for one hour.

Freeze breast milk in two and four ounce containers. No milk will be wasted because the caregiver can thaw only what the baby is expected to use at one feeding and then thaw more if the baby wants more. It is normal for the milk to separate into milk and cream. It should be given a gentle shake before the feeding. It also is normal for human milk to have a bluish, yellowish or brownish color.

Rancid Milk

In rare cases, some mothers produce milk high in lipase, the enzyme that breaks down fat. When this happens the mother's milk becomes rancid when refrigerated or frozen. Mothers should freeze several test samples of their milk and then thaw them after a week to see if they smell bad. To inactivate the lipase, the milk can be heated to a scald immediately after collecting it. Quickly cool it and then freeze it.

Formula Supplement

You can feed your baby formula as a supplement to breastfeeding without ill effects. Prepare the formula as directed.

Whichever method you prefer, it is a good idea to keep a can of powdered formula on the top shelf in the kitchen to relieve a common fear which can inhibit the milk flow: "What happens if I get sick or have to go to the hospital? Who will feed the baby?" The formula is there for emergencies.

Nursing and Medications

Nursing mothers frequently call their pediatrician or family practitioner with questions about nursing and medications. The following are some general guidelines. If you have any questions regarding a specific medication, please call your pediatrician or family practitioner.

Pain Medications: Aspirin, a salicylate, can have a tendency to cause adverse effects in the infant, especially if used at higher doses. Also, due to the unknown link of salicylates with Reyes syndrome, the use of aspirin is not warranted. Acetaminophen (Tylenol, Anacin 3,) ibuprofen (Advil, Motrin, Nuprin, Medipren, Motrin IB) and naproxen (Naprosyn, Alleve) can be taken as needed and have no effect on the baby.

Medication that contains codeine or its derivatives can be taken in limited amounts. If you must be on a narcotic drug for a prolonged time, discuss this with your pediatrician or family practitioner.

Cold Medications: Most antihistamine or decongestant cold and cough medications sold over-the-counter do not cause serious problems for the baby. Side effects (especially with those drugs containing phenylpropylalanine and pseudephedrine) can include making the baby drowsy, restless or irritable. Antihistamines can decrease milk volume. These drugs should always be taken after nursing. Long acting preparations should be avoided.

Antibiotics: Although most antibiotics can be taken by nursing mothers, there are some exceptions. Sulfa drugs (like Bactrim, Septra, Gantrisin) should be used with caution if the baby is jaundiced. Tetracycline can be taken for short courses of less than three weeks. Longer exposure puts the baby at risk of reduced bone growth and dental staining. Drugs that should not be used while nursing include: Chloramphenicol, Quinolones (Cipro.)

Asthma Medications: Theophylline and albuterol (Ventolin, Proventil) can be taken. Some infants will show signs of irritability or sleeplessness if the mother is taking these drugs.

Steroids: Courses of steroids can be taken while breastfeeding.

Birth Control Pills: Birth control pills can be taken while nursing. Some estrogen/progesterone combinations may decrease milk production. Discuss this with your family practitioner or obstetrician.

Anti-Depressants: In certain situations, depending on the drug being taken, nursing can be continued with close supervision.

Alcohol: Alcohol can be consumed in limited amounts. An occasional drink is not a problem but regular use and intoxication can cause serious side effects.

Caffeine: Amounts should be limited because some infants show signs of restlessness and sleeplessness.

Nicotine: Smoking and nursing are not compatible. Large doses of nicotine have caused serious side effects in newborns. Second-hand smoke has been shown to increase the risk of asthma and other "wheezing" conditions in growing lungs.

Cocaine: **Cocaine should absolutely not be used while nursing.** Serious cocaine intoxications have occurred in infants. Cocaine is a dangerous drug and should **never** be used.

Amphetamines, Heroin, Marijuana, PCP, Ecstasy or any other designer drugs: **These drugs should never be used.**

If you have any questions about the drugs discussed here or others not listed, please call your physician.

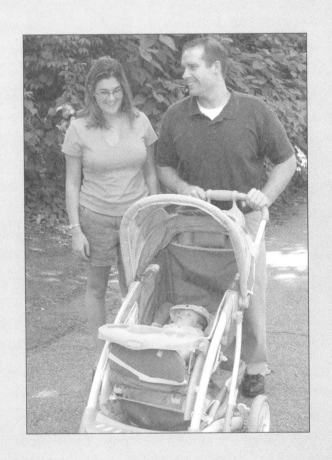

"I remember leaving the hospital...thinking,
Wait, are they going to let me just walk off with
him? I don't know beans about babies!
I don't have a license to do this (we're) just amateurs."

—Anne Tyler (Author)

"You know more than you think you do."

—Dr. Benjamin Spock
(Pediatrician and Author)
Baby and Child Care, 1945

Your Newborn at Home

Suggested Supplies

Car seat (Mandatory)

Plain, unscented soaps (such as the brands Dove or Basis)

Non-stinging baby shampoo (such as the brands Johnson & Johnson, Baby Magic)

Non-scented lotion (such as the brands Lubriderm, Eucerin, Moisturel)

Ointment (such as the brands A & D or Vaseline)

Desitin, Balmex or any other ointment with zinc oxide

Baby oil (for treating cradle cap)

Rubbing alcohol (for cord care)

Cotton balls and sterile gauze

Q-tips

Toothbrush (soft bristle) for hair care

Detergent (such as the brands Cheer, Dreft, or Tide powders or Cheerfree or Tidefree liquids—best for sensitive skin as per dermatologists)

Saltwater nose drops or spray (such as the brands Nasal, Ocean)

Nasal aspirator

Measuring spoon or measuring syringe

Rectal thermometer (mercury or digital)

Bottles or sterile bags (such as Playtex or Evenflow)

Nipples

Pacifier (make certain that, if you use a pacifier, it is made in one piece)

Assorted bath towels and cloths

Undershirts ("Onesies")

Cloth diapers (good for everything!)

Disposable diapers

Mattress pads

Crib sheets

Wipes (we recommend that you use unscented ones)

Cold-water vaporizers (avoid ultrasonic or warm mist humidifiers)

Diaper bag and changing pad

Optional

Swing (battery operated ones are great!)

Carrier (such as "Snugli")

Intercom or monitor

Safety

DVD Chap 7

Important Safety Notes:

- Never put a rear-facing car seat on the front passenger side.

- Crib slats should be less than 2–3/8 inches apart.

- Never let your baby sleep on a pillow or bean bag mattress.

- Water temperature should be set less than 120° F.

- Baby should be positioned for sleep on back or side.

- Never leave your baby alone on an elevated surface.

- Never shake your baby.

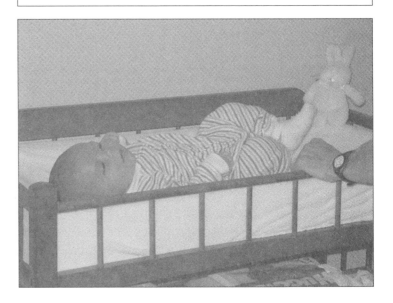

Car Seats

"First Ride, Safe Ride!" You will need a child safety car seat to take the baby home from the hospital.

Make certain that the child safety car seat faces backward during infancy. According to AAA, NEVER install a rear-facing child safety car seat in the front seat of a car equipped with passenger side air bags.

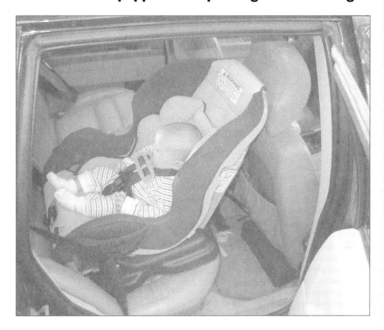

You also want to be certain that the car seat is reclined, so that the baby doesn't fall forward. Follow manufacturer's suggestions for securing the car seat in your vehicle. Many car dealerships and some local police stations now provide free checks of your car seat's position.

Cribs

Crib slats should be less than 2–3/8 inches apart. Crib sides should be up whenever the baby is left unattended. Crib bumpers should be used. Never use old cribs (antiques or cribs made before 1984) unless the slats are less than 2-3/8 inches apart and have not been painted with lead-based paint (as the baby gets older he may chew on the crib's sides.) The crib mattress should fit snugly against all sides. Do not use a pillow until your baby is able to turn himself fully. And never use sheepskin pads, waterbed mattresses or beanbags.

Falls

Never leave the baby alone on any elevated surface or on the bed even for a second. This includes infant chairs on tabletops.

Fire

Install smoke detectors in the home.

Jewelry

Avoid jewelry on your baby especially necklaces as these may pose a danger of strangulation and choking. Bracelets with medals can also pose a choking hazard if they become loose.

Although in some cultures, early ear piercing is performed routinely, ears should not be pierced until the child is at least four to six months of age after the cartilage is formed. That being said, if it is necessary to pierce a baby's ear, you should be aware of the following problems that could occur. The earring post can be grasped by the baby and pulled completely through the ear, leaving a laceration. The scar can lead to deformity of the earlobe. Also, an infant may remove the earring and put it in her mouth. This may cause choking and aspiration. So avoid hoops and use solid post 24k gold earring. Have a doctor's office do the piercing if possible.

Pacifiers
Use only one-piece designs, which cannot separate. Dentists recommend this orthodontic shape. **Never hang a pacifier around the baby's neck.** You can use special clips designed to attach to clothing.

Sleep Position
Because of concerns that sleep position may be related to Sudden Infant Death Syndrome (SIDS), the American Academy of Pediatrics has made the following recommendation:

Healthy infants should be positioned on their side or back when being put down for sleep.

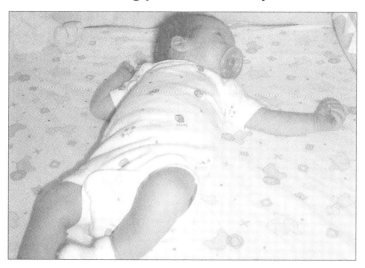

For infants with certain medical conditions, your family practitioner or pediatrician may recommend another position.

Suffocation

Avoid purchasing pillows that conform to the baby's body, such as beanbags. A number of these products were responsible for several infant deaths due to suffocation. Although these products have been recalled, there still may be some in circulation. They were marketed under the following names: Mother's Helper, Gold Bug Support Sacks, Cozy Cushions, Cozy Baby Pillows, Baby Minder, and Baby Sak. Waterbed mattresses have also been linked to some infant deaths.

Toys

Avoid mobiles or toys with long strings, cradle gyms that are loose, and any small objects in order to avoid the danger of strangulation.

Water Temperature

Set the water heater thermostat at less than 120° F to avoid scalding in the event that the hot tap water should go on by accident while bathing. Do not put the baby under running water for the same reason.

Never leave the baby unattended in even the smallest amount of water or for what might seem to be even the shortest period of time!

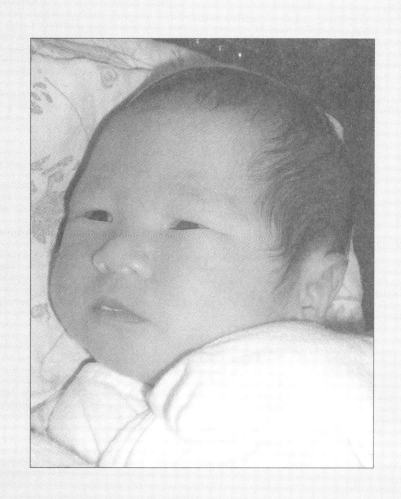

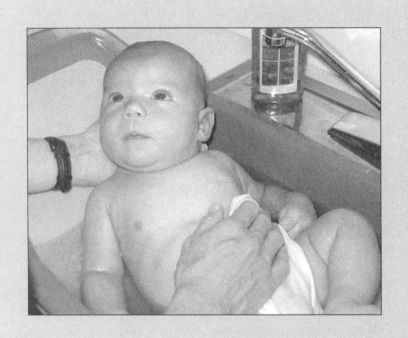

"Parents don't come full bloom at the birth of the
first baby. In fact parenting is about growing...
our own growing as much as our children's
growing and that kind of growing happens little by little."

–Fred Rogers
(TV Personality and Author)
The Mister Rogers Parenting Book, 2002

Your Baby from A to Z

DVD Chap 3

Bathing

You may bathe your baby once a day. Baths can be as infrequent as two to three times a week if excessive dryness is a problem. This is especially the case in the winter months. Before the cord falls off, sponge baths are recommended. I recommend using an unscented soap for the infant's sensitive skin. Normally, it is not necessary to use anything but warm water on the baby's face. However, if the baby develops "neonatal acne," you may gently wash the face with soap, but be sure to rinse well.

DVD Chap 1

Behavior

Infants at this age can focus clearly on an object eight inches from their eyes. This is exactly the distance between the baby and the mother's (or father's) face during feeding. Babies react to the human face (or even a drawing of a face) during this time period. Smiling and making faces at your new arrival is the best stimulation you can do—and it's fun too!

At this age, babies are good imitators and they will try to mimic your facial movements (open mouth, stick out tongue.) In addition to the human face, babies also enjoy sharply contrasting colors, large squares, bright lights and round shapes. Moving objects are more attractive than still ones.

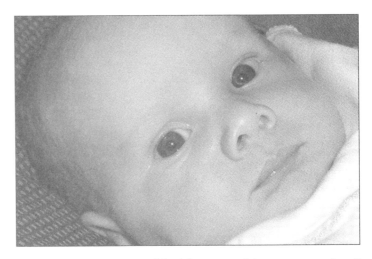

Touching, cuddling and holding are all important stimuli to your baby. They are a form of communication, which will often calm a fussy baby.

The startle reflex occurs whenever the baby hears a loud noise or moves suddenly downward. Both arms will move out and then in, and the baby may grimace or cry. This is a normal reaction.

Babies usually smile by two months of age. This can occur earlier. I will never argue with the grandmother who claims the baby smiled at one week of age. Most babies are at least six weeks old before they can smile in response to something (such as another smiling face.)

When a baby is crying and upset, he will have some capacity to quiet himself by hand-to-mouth activities. This may range from brief swipes of the hand to the mouth to actual thumb sucking. You should be able to use some of this information as well as your own observations to console your baby and to interact with him in a positive, stimulating way. Be careful not to over stimulate! Remember to enjoy your baby!

Birthmarks

There are two types of birthmarks that can first appear when the baby is between two or three weeks old. These are called hemangiomas and they can either be a deep red color (strawberry hemangioma) or a deep blue color (blueberry hemangioma.) Strawberry hemangiomas are the most common.

Both types of hemangiomas can commonly grow to be the size of an olive and can be raised up off the surface of the skin. In most cases, they do not cause any problems and disappear by age three or four years without treatment. There are new laser treatments available but these are used only in certain situations. If your child develops one of these birthmarks, discuss it with your pediatrician or family practitioner and he/she will determine appropriate treatment with you.

So-called "stork bites" are pink areas found on the forehead, upper eyelids and back of the neck. They are a collection of tiny blood vessels and usually disappear by a year of age. The neck mark will probably stay longer, only to become hidden by hair. This, too, will fade over time.

Breasts

Both newborn girls and boys can have enlarged breasts during the time they are exposed to maternal hormones. Sometimes a "milky" discharge can be expressed. A breast-fed baby may have this phenomenon a bit longer than bottle-fed babies. There is no need for concern or treatment. Occasionally, one breast may appear red or inflamed. Notify your pediatrician or family practitioner if this occurs to assure that no infection is present.

Colic

The causes of colic remain a mystery. It is thought to be spasms of abdominal pain, perhaps related to an immature gastrointestinal system and the presence of gas. Sometimes an allergy to cow's milk proteins or soy-based formulas can cause colic-like symptoms. Breast-fed babies can get colic, too. Some breastfeeding mothers report a dramatic improvement when milk, milk products, chocolate, fruit, eggs, caffeine, onions, or supplemental irons are eliminated from their diet. You will have to use the trial-and-error approach. However, it may take as long as a week before results are seen. The treatment for colic is not easy and requires patience on your part and your pediatrician or family practitioner. Happily, it is a self-limited problem that is usually resolved by the third month. However, it can be a long three months.

If the baby has long crying periods when nothing seems to calm him down, call your family practitioner or pediatrician to discuss the possibility that this may be colic. He/she may make suggestions as to what can be

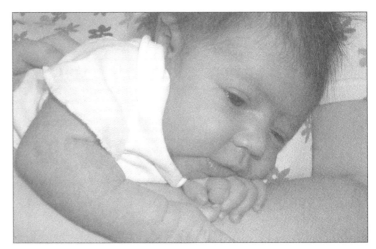

done. You can try rocking, swinging (either in your arms or in a wind up swing,) rhythmic patting on the back, music with a beat, a car ride, a gentle massage of the stomach, letting the vacuum cleaner run (some respond to the noise,) use of a front carrier, or putting the baby in an infant seat on top of a gently running clothes dryer. But remember to stay with the baby to avoid falling!

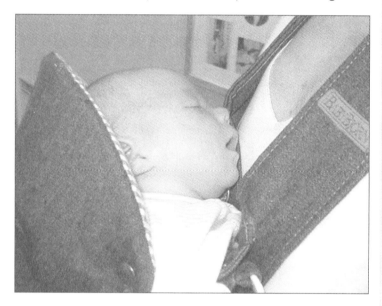

Constipation

If no stool is passed for more than four days, if the stools are hard and ball-shaped, or if the baby appears to be in pain when passing the stool, this may represent constipation. If there is blood on the diaper or in the stool, please notify your pediatrician or family practitioner so he/she can make sure it is simply local bleeding from passing a hard, formed stool.

After a four day period with no stool, I recommend that you insert 1/4 of an infant glycerin suppository into the rectum. This usually will produce immediate results. Follow this treatment by beginning to give the baby a mixture of one ounce of prune juice or pear juice to one ounce of water each day until a regular bowel pattern is attained.

Avoid the regular use of suppositories, baby enemas, rectal stimulation, or home remedies.

If constipation is accompanied by vomiting, or other signs of illness are present in the baby, call your pediatrician or family practitioner immediately.

Cord Care

DVD Chap 3

The cord will normally fall off sometime between one and four weeks of age. You can facilitate this by keeping it as dry as possible: give sponge baths, fold the diaper below the level of the cord and apply alcohol twice a day to the entire cord area. It is not necessary to apply alcohol with every diaper change.

If the cord becomes messy, use alcohol or hydrogen peroxide to clean it. There may be some spotting of blood on the diaper or around the cord (especially as it

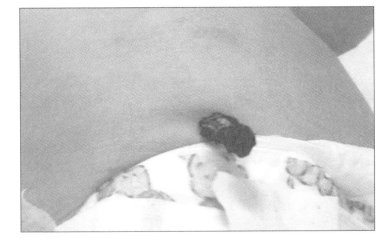

is getting ready to fall off). Do not be alarmed by this. However, if the bleeding is continuous or if the cord develops a foul odor or you notice pus around the cord, call your pediatrician or family practitioner for treatment.

Cradle Cap

Occasionally, a baby develops cradle cap. This occurs when the scalp develops flaking or scaliness. If cradle cap is present, you can apply baby oil with a soft bristle toothbrush to remove the scales. Use the baby oil daily before shampooing until the condition resolves. If, after one week, this does not work, add a capful of Selsun Blue (or similar) shampoo to a bottle of baby shampoo. Use this mixture for the daily shampoo. Cradle cap may sometimes take weeks or months to resolve. It is almost always gone by the first birthday.

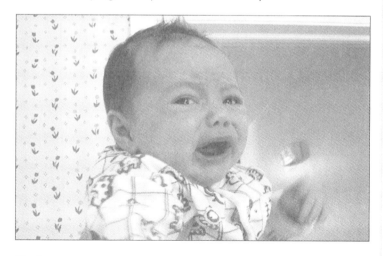

Crying

Crying is your baby's only form of communication. In a short time, you will be able to interpret your baby's cries and recognize which one means hunger, which one means wet, etc. Crying does not always mean hunger, particularly if the baby was fed within two hours. Typically the amount of crying increases during the first two to three months of life. Many babies have a "fussy

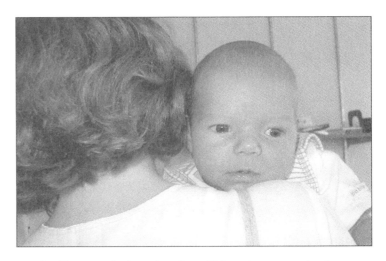

period" once during the day. Often it occurs in the evening between 5 p.m. and 11 p.m., just when the rest of the family is settling down to a nice dinner or preparing for bed! Nothing seems to calm the baby down but rocking, cuddling and attention. This is not colic, but can be just as frustrating. Fortunately, the "fussy period" lasts only a few weeks (but can recur just before a new developmental phase is about to begin.)

You cannot spoil a newborn infant! Any cry is a signal of anxiety, distress or pain and should be responded to if it continues longer than five minutes. Even just touching your body and feeling warmth can calm a baby down. If the crying continues, at least you have responded to the baby and this will help instill a sense of trust in your child. If you need or want to, there is no harm in taking an infant to your bed, and this may help everyone sleep better.

Detergent
Use a detergent like Cheer, Tide or Dreft powders or Cheerfree or Tidefree liquids that are the least irritating to skin. Avoid soap detergents for they will remove the flame retardant from your baby's clothing.

Diaper Rash

If a rash is developing, change the baby's diaper frequently and immediately after soiling. Whenever possible, rinse the skin after a bowel movement. Avoid occlusive diaper covers, especially at night. Apply barrier cream (such as Desitin or Balmex) liberally with each diaper change. These protect the skin by sealing out humidity and irritating factors that may be present in urine or stool. These also reduce friction. You don't have to remove all of the previously applied ointment with each diaper change. Superficial cleansing followed by another application of ointment is sufficient. If diaper rash persists more than a few days, a yeast infection may have developed. Try adding an anti-fungal cream such as the brand Lotrimen (sold over the counter as Athlete's Foot cream) with each diaper change. Sometimes a prescription called Nystatin is needed.

Diapering

DVD Chap 3

The diaper area should be cleaned thoroughly after the baby has a stool or urinates. A wet washcloth can be used. Some people prefer baby wipes. Since wipes usually contain lanolin or are scented, they may be irritating to a newborn's tender skin. You may wish to wait until the baby is one month or older before using these, or look for an unscented variety.

Change your baby frequently and immediately after soiling. Using soap in the diaper area with each change is unnecessary and can remove protective oils from the skin, making it more susceptible to problems. Therefore, use water alone or wipes containing non-soap cleansers and moisturizers. Wipes should be unscented and alcohol-free.

To reduce friction in the diaper area, an ointment like A & D Ointment or Vaseline can be used with each diaper change and Desitin or Balmex can be applied if a rash is developing. Avoid baby powder. It serves no

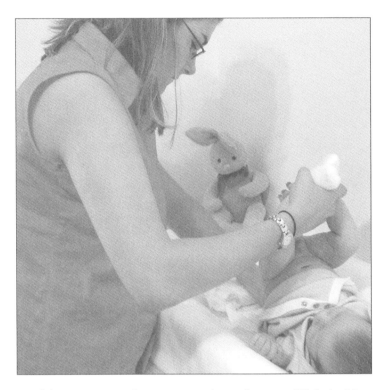

useful purpose and may cause lung damage if inhaled by the baby. Cornstarch is safer and does not contain the nutrient protein and oil that encourages yeast to grow. Disposable diapers have a smooth inner lining and no powder is necessary. If using cloth diapers, wash with a fabric softener. You may apply a little corn starch to the cloth, but do not sprinkle near the baby's face.

If you choose to use disposable diapers, the brand you use does not really matter. You may switch brands if a sensitivity develops.

It is no secret that we are running out of landfill in this country. Disposable diapers are a major convenience but are also a major burden on the environment. The expense of a diaper service is about equal to the cost of buying disposable diapers. If you purchase and launder your own non-disposable diapers, the cost drops considerably. Cloth covers, which hold the diaper in place with Velcro closures, are now available.

Dressing

Dress your baby as you would dress yourself. Avoid overdressing, especially in warm weather. If the baby is overdressed the body temperature may rise. This can result in prickly heat rash. A hat should be used in summer to avoid sun and in the winter to avoid heat loss. Avoid multiple blankets at night. In general, 100% cotton fabrics seem to be best for your newborn's sensitive skin. Synthetic fabrics can cause more sweating and can be more irritating. Note, however, that pajamas are always made of synthetic materials, which are flame retardant for safety.

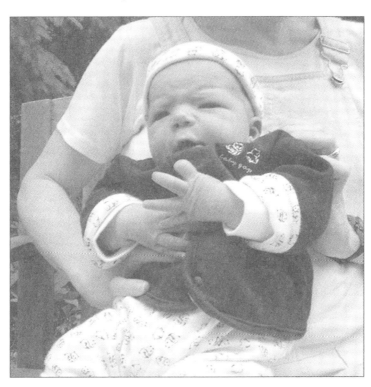

Eye Color

Those deep blue eyes may be an awesome brown by nine months. As with hair color, eye color is transient and the definitive color may not be present until nine to 12 months of age.

Genital Care

Boys

For little boys who are circumcised, apply A & D Ointment or Vaseline to the circumcision site for a few days. Wash as usual. As normal healing progresses, a band of yellow healing skin will develop and then begin to peel.

For little boys who are uncircumcised, the baby's penis needs to be cleaned with soap and water only. There is no need to retract the foreskin. (In fact, to attempt to retract the foreskin of a newborn could be traumatic and cause pain and bleeding.) The natural separation of the foreskin from the glands of the penis may take months or even years to develop. While most foreskins can be retracted by age five years, there are times when this does not occur until adolescence. Smegma, a white "cheesy" substance, may accumulate under the foreskin. This is only sloughed skin cells and is easily cleaned.

Girls

Little girls frequently have smegma, too, which accumulates around the hood of the clitoris, and white mucous in the vaginal area. This can be removed gently with a washcloth or with a Q-tip during the bath, if desired.

Vaginal bleeding may occur occasionally during the first week of life. This is a result of exposure to the mother's hormones and is no cause for alarm.

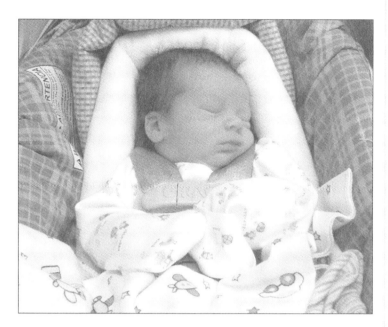

Going Out

After the first week of life, the normal full-term infant can adjust to most temperature changes. Depending on the weather, it is safe to take the baby out for short walks or brief trips. Dress your baby appropriately for the weather. Use discretion with strangers who just cannot resist picking up and holding your baby. Avoid malls or crowded areas for the first two months until the baby's immune system matures.

Hair

Your baby's hair should be washed at bath time with a gentle baby shampoo. Don't be afraid to wash over the baby's fontanelle (soft spot). It is a very tough membrane, and is not hurt by touching or washing. Although you are in love with the little blond, redhead or dark black mop-top, it is true that most babies lose this hair over the next few months, and by one to two years of age may have a completely different hair color and texture, which you will love just as much.

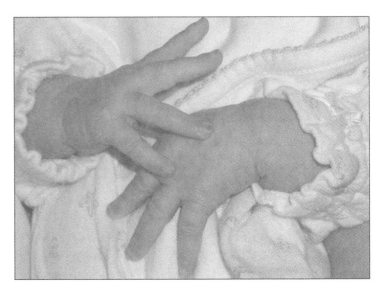

Nails

Fingernails can scratch the baby's face or eyes and should be trimmed. It is not always easy to do this because the nails are so small and because they are very soft at this stage. There are a variety of techniques people try, including cutting with a scissor, filing with an emery board, or using specially made baby nail clippers. I do not recommend biting the baby's nails off. The best time to do any of these is when the baby is sleeping. Occasionally, toenails can appear ingrown. Have your pediatrician or family practitioner take a look at them if this occurs.

In the event that the baby does scratch himself, do not worry. These will heal quickly without a scar. It is not necessary to put mittens or socks over your baby's hands and it interferes with an important part of their development. Their hands are their way of exploring the world—**do not cover them.**

Neonatal Acne

From about two to ten weeks of age there is a rash on the face and neck that comes and goes spontaneously. It is thought to be associated with hormonal changes as the infant has been exposed to his mother's hormones. This rash is red, raised and "acne like." The rash changes from day to day. It is worse when the baby is kept too hot or has been crying. Gentle cleansing with a basic soap may help. Avoid scrubbing and lotions.

Pacifiers

Babies have a tremendous sucking need that cannot be filled by feeding alone. If a pacifier is not provided, the baby will suck fingers, hands, etc. There is no harm in introducing a pacifier at this age, and it may provide a way for the baby to relieve tensions. Usually, the pacifier can be removed at age four or five months, when the sucking need diminishes. If you decide to use a pacifier, I recommend a one piece, orthodontic pacifier.

Never tie the pacifier around the baby's neck!

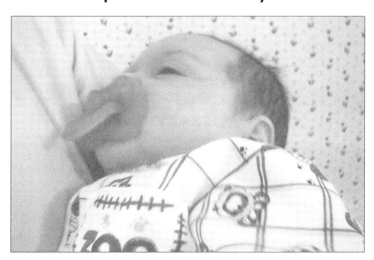

Room Temperature

The baby's room should not be overheated. The temperature should be kept between 68° and 72° F. If temperature cannot be controlled, the baby should be undressed as much as possible in a warm room and bundled in a cold room—especially during the first week of life. Temperature changes from warm to cold may be upsetting to an infant's equilibrium. When part of his body is exposed to a real temperature change, his whole body changes color in an effort to equalize the local temperature change. The baby may even become upset and cry in order to improve his body's circulation and to protest. When he is warm he quiets down again.

Skin

General principles for skin care are as follows:

- Avoid scented creams or lotions, which may irritate the baby's skin. Let the baby smell like a baby.

- Use an unscented soap. Some brands include Dove or Basis.

- Avoid baby oil or Vaseline on the face.

- Avoid all powders, especially talc, which can cause serious lung problems if accidentally inhaled by the baby.

- Use a non-irritating lubricant, (brands such as Lubriderm, Moisturel or Eucerin cream) on the body, particularly after bathing. Corn starch can be used in warm weather in the creases of fat folds especially if sweating is a problem.

- Use a simple ointment, such as the brand A & D, in the diaper area.

The newborn skin is normally dry, peels easily and is very sensitive. A variety of common newborn rashes can occur during the first few days of life. Most rashes require no special care and resolve within a few days.

White cheesy material tends to accumulate in the creases of the newborn's skin especially under their arms. Again, you can apply baby oil to a Q-tip and clean out as much as possible.

Sleep

Newborns sleep most of the day with alert times increasing in frequency and duration during the next few months. Babies usually do not sleep through the night until two to four months of age (perhaps longer for breast-fed babies.)

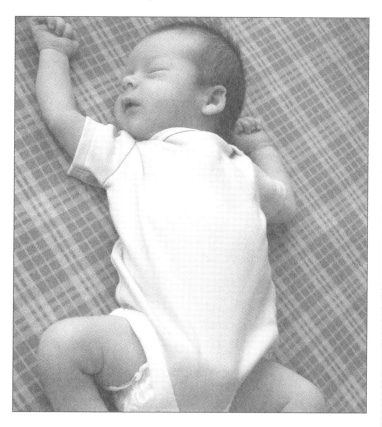

Sleep Position

Because of recent concerns that sleep position may be related to Sudden Infant Death Syndrome (SIDS), the American Academy of Pediatrics made the following recommendation: **Healthy infants should be positioned on their side or back when being put down for sleep.** For infants with certain medical conditions, your pediatrician or family practitioner may recommend another position.

Sound, Reaction To

Research has shown that newborns exhibit more consistent quieting and alerting to a soft, high pitched voice than to a low one. Thus, it might seem that the baby has a preference for his mother's voice over his father's. At least this justifies why people talk to babies in high squeaky voices!

Stools

The number of bowel movements a baby has can vary greatly. What is important is not the number of stools per day but rather the consistency of the stool.

Breast-fed babies will typically have thin, seedy yellow to green stools. These stools can be very frequent, sometimes occurring with every feeding. The stools may seem "explosive" in nature.

Bottle-fed babies will tend to have a more formed or pasty stool, often more green in color than breast-fed babies. Bottle-fed babies will stool less often than their breast-fed counterparts (usually one to two stools per day although stooling varies from baby to baby).

Some babies, even those who are breastfeeding, may have only one or two stools per day or even one stool every three or four days. This is not necessarily constipation, and no intervention is necessary if the baby is not in discomfort and the stool is soft. It is normal for babies to grunt, groan and turn red in the face during the passage of a stool. This apparent straining is necessary to push the stool out without the benefit of gravity. This also does not mean the baby is constipated.

Far too much attention is given to the color of a baby's stools. Aside from black, red or white any other color is normal—this includes green, yellow brown or variations thereof.

Stuffiness

Stuffiness or mucous in the nose is very common at this age. It can be due to dry air, dust, or wool lint from fuzzy blankets. Spitting up adds to the irritation with milk residue left in the back of the nose. This can be irritating and needs to be cleared away by sneezing and coughing. A cool-mist humidifier in the room helps. Using a cool-mist humidifier is especially important in the winter when the dry heat inside and the cold air outside make matters worse. The mucous and milk in the back of the nose may make the breathing noisy. This does not harm the baby.

Sudden Infant Death Syndrome (SIDS)

The occurrence of SIDS is rare during the first month of life, but peaks between two and four months of age before declining in the remainder of the first year of life. Although the cause is still being actively researched, the *Back to Sleep* campaign, which advises parents to have their babies sleep on their backs, has dramatically reduced the incidence. Other factors that have been shown to increase a baby's risk of SIDS are maternal smoking during pregnancy, sleeping on a soft surface, and overheating (this includes over-wrapping or swaddling a baby). *See the Reference and Resources section for more information.*

Sun Exposure

The newborn should not be in direct sunlight. If this cannot be avoided, the baby should not be without a hat and tee shirt. According to the American Academy of Pediatrics, sunscreen should be used when there is a risk that your infant will have a sunburn. Below six months of age, sunscreen should be applied in small amounts to areas of the body not protected by clothing, especially the face and back of hands. The sunscreen should be PABA free with UVA and UVB protection and at least SPF 15 but not more than 30. If you are unsure about which product to select, you can check with your pediatrician or family practitioner.

Urine

The baby should urinate several times a day. This indicates that the baby is receiving enough fluid to drink. A little boy's urine stream should arch in the air. If you are observing this, take cover! If you do not notice this, please tell your pediatrician or family practitioner.

Visiting

Everyone wants to see and hold your new baby. While this may be wonderful for the visitors, it may be harmful to the baby. Anyone with a respiratory or stomach virus should avoid close contact with the baby. Hands should be washed before handling the infant (this includes the baby's parents and siblings if they are coming in from the outside). Large parties and crowds of people—such as at shopping malls and supermarkets—should be avoided whenever possible until after two months of age. You may take the baby out of the house for a walk as long as you avoid crowds.

Close contact should be limited to parents, siblings and grandparents. Pets and young children should be supervised around the baby. You must be firm on this issue. You can use your pediatrician or family practitioner to take the blame!

Vitamins

Most formula fed infants, drinking at least 17 oz. per day will get their daily vitamin requirement from formula. If you are breastfeeding, the Academy of Pediatrics recommends a vitamin supplement containing Vitamin D to prevent rickets in infancy, a bone softening disease caused by Vitamin D deficiency. However, most women if they get 10-15 minutes of natural sunlight 2-3 times per week will produce adequate levels of Vitamin D.

If you are breastfeeding and are in situations that limit the amount of sunlight that you take in through your skin, you may be at risk for Vitamin D deficiency, and therefore so may your infant. Living in urban areas or high latitudes, staying indoors most of the time, or covering most of your skin with clothing while outside are all Vitamin D deficiency risk factors. If you feel you may be at risk, then discuss with your doctor about the need for Vitamin supplements.

Infant vitamins usually come as a tri-vitamin containing Vitamins A, C and D or as a multivitamin, which includes the B-complexes as well. Your pediatrician will help make the decision about the need for vitamins and which type might be best for your baby.

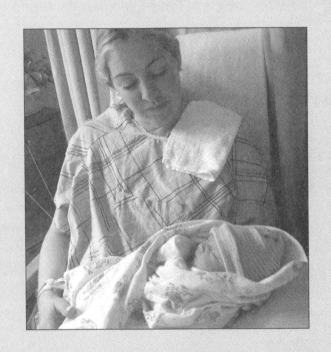

"Attachment to a baby is a long-term process,
not a single, magical moment. The opportunity for bonding
at birth may be compared to falling in love——staying in
love takes longer and demands more work."

—Dr. T. Berry Brazelton
(Pediatrician)
Touchpoints, 1992

Family and the Newborn

Mothers

Baby Blues

Although the birth of a child is supposed to be a happy time, for some women it may be just the opposite as they are suddenly overcome by feelings of depression or anxiety.

The most common form of postpartum depression is the well known "baby blues." This occurs in the first weeks following the birth of the baby and lasts only a few days. The mother finds herself feeling sad, irritable or confused and has crying spells, difficulty sleeping or loss of appetite.

Symptoms are most intense within the first week after childbirth. This occurs in 10–16% of new mothers and resolves without treatment. The cause is suspected to be hormonal (similar to premenstrual syndrome).

What Can You Do?

If the symptoms last only for a few days, you need only to let it pass. If you feel like crying—cry. It helps if your spouse or family members recognize that this is a normal phase. Insensitive comments such as "Just snap out of it" or "How can you be sad with such a beautiful baby?" do not help the situation. If the symptoms last longer than two weeks, please notify your obstetrician. Prolonged baby blues may need to be treated with medication.

Postpartum Depression

This form of post-childbirth depression is less common than the "baby blues" but can affect 10–20% of new mothers in some form during the first year. The severity of the depression varies from mild to severe. The symptoms of postpartum depression usually begin one to four months after delivery and may last up to one year if left untreated.

The symptoms of postpartum depression include the well-known signs of general depression. These include: overwhelming sadness, crying spells, loss of appetite, difficulty sleeping and an inability to feel happy with the new baby or with other aspects of life.

Other symptoms can be the symptoms of anxiety. These symptoms are more subtle but may include a sense of overwhelming uneasiness or panic attacks. When this happens, the person usually describes a feeling of impending doom, often accompanied by chest pain, shortness of breath, and/or rapid heart rate.

The cause of postpartum depression is not well known. It is most likely related to a combination of hormonal and psychological factors. The stress of caring for a new baby who may be difficult only adds to the problem, as does sleep deprivation.

Many women do not seek help because they are ashamed that they are not experiencing the "joys of motherhood." These women hide their symptoms, but continue to feel miserable inside. This disorder is treatable, and it is important to treat. Studies by the American Academy of Pediatrics have shown that newborns (and infants) are affected by a mother's chronically depressed mood. If you experience any of the symptoms listed or you just don't feel "right," let your physician know. Tell your obstetrician, family practitioner or pediatrician. *(See the Reference and Resource section for more information.)*

Bonding and Attachment

Many mothers believe that there is a magical "bonding" that occurs immediately following the birth. They are supposed to feel "totally in love" with their new baby without reservation and they are very concerned if this does not occur right away. If a separation occurs after delivery (for example, if mother or baby becomes ill) or if a baby is adopted, some mothers are afraid that bonding will not occur normally.

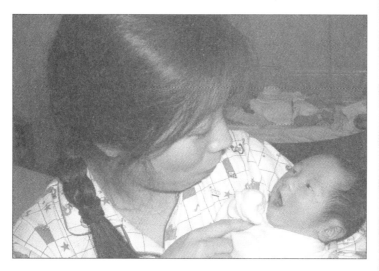

We now know that bonding and attachment to your new infant is a very complicated process that often takes some time. Although some mothers report feelings that occur after delivery, most mothers describe this as a slower process. As you begin to feel better, the hormones settle down and the shock of having a baby begins to wear off, you will begin the attachment process to your new infant. The same is true for babies who come to you through adoption. The process of bonding to your infant is unique to every family.

Stress and the New Mother

As you prepare to bring your new baby home, you are probably making lists of things that have to be done, or making arrangements for relatives and friends to visit. If you have always been a very organized person who likes to get things done, you may believe that the baby won't change this. You may plan activities and projects at your old pace.

Try to remember that you have just had a baby. If you have had a Caesarian section you have also just had major surgery. You need time to recover.

The first two weeks should be a restful time (longer for a C-section). First of all, your body needs time to heal. You may still be in pain from the episiotomy, hemorrhoids or sutures. You may be anemic from blood loss. The new baby will not be sleeping through the night and neither will you for a few weeks. If you are breastfeeding, your body must adjust to this additional energy drain.

Please remember—You simply will not be able to do everything. If you know this ahead of time, hopefully you will not be too hard on yourself.

The housework can wait—or others can do it for you. The family can either cook for themselves, or rely on frozen dinners or meals prepared by friends or relatives. The laundry can wait or someone else can do it.

The second thing to consider is that you need time to get to know your new baby. Some authors have referred to this period as your "babymoon." You wouldn't take your parents or friends on your honeymoon would you? You needed that time to get to know each other without anyone else around. Bonding is not always automatic. You need to be together.

Keep your social life to a minimum for the first two weeks. Stay in bed if you want. If you are nursing, you may find that this helps your milk flow. Your body will soon feel more normal and your energy level will return after a month or two. This will happen sooner if you take it easy in the beginning.

Your life is going to change and so will your priorities. The concept of "Super-Mom" is gone. Whether you plan to return to work outside the home or become a full-time mom, life will never be the same. You just cannot do everything you did before the baby was born. There will be days when getting through a shower will seem like a great accomplishment!

Helping Hands

A baby is like a "people magnet." Everyone wants to see the new baby. Well-meaning friends and relatives bring presents. But as I have mentioned, you need time for your "babymoon." Not everyone needs to visit in the first few weeks. The baby will still be as cute as ever later on. You will enjoy the company of friends more when you are feeling better.

Trust how you are feeling. Every woman reacts to childbirth in her own way. If you are feeling great and enjoy company, invite people over. If you are feeling tired or not in the mood for company, people will understand.

Although the help from relatives who may live with you for a time after the baby can be invaluable, let them know that you need time with the baby. They can help with the housework, cooking or other children. Parents should do most of the care for the baby. A sensitive grandmother will know this and be supportive as you learn to care for the baby.

Fathers

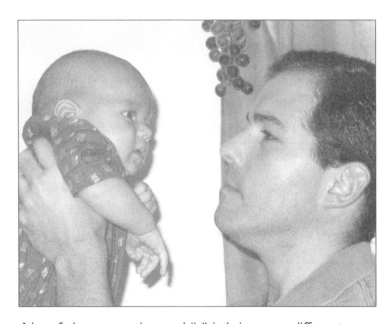

New fathers experience childbirth in many different ways. Although they don't go through the physical pain of labor and delivery, they are right there watching someone they love go through a painful and often frightening experience. They may be filled with emotions they don't understand and yet no one is asking them how they feel. All the focus is on the new mother and baby. It is easy for fathers to feel confused and left out. Talking with other new fathers can help. Even just knowing that others are feeling the same way can make you feel more at ease. Many men do not have a great deal of experience with small babies and are afraid to hold or feed them. If you feel nervous, have someone show you how to hold the baby. Babies enjoy being held by their fathers as much as they enjoy their mothers.

You must be informed about breastfeeding so that you can be supportive. You can participate by making your wife comfortable or getting her the glass of water or juice that she needs with each nursing.

If the baby is bottle-feeding, or if breastfeeding will be supplemented with a bottle, feeding time is a great chance to get in on the act. Learn how to prepare the bottle and feed the baby. Then ask your wife to leave the room while you feed the baby. You will be more relaxed and will have time alone with your baby to get to know each other. It also gives Mom a break, which she will appreciate soon enough.

Siblings

If this is your second child here are some ideas that might help your older child adjust to the new baby.

Most children will have feelings of jealousy towards the new baby and anger towards you. It's normal for the child to display these feelings and you can help by letting the child express his or her feelings without recrimination. It's important for the child to know that you still love them even if they have mixed feelings.

Do not leave small toddlers alone with the new baby.

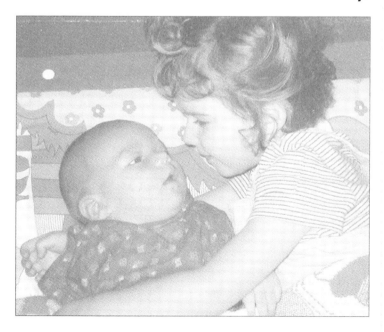

It is not uncommon for a toddler to hit or try to hurt the newborn. Some experts recommend having another family member carry the infant into the house, leaving the mother free to reconnect with the siblings.

Buy a present for your older child and give it to your older child "from the baby" when you come home from the hospital.

Often, the first months are not a problem. Older siblings enjoy all the visitors, the gifts and the excitement that accompanies a new baby. Jealousy and resentment may not appear until later on, when they realize the new baby isn't "going back."

Encourage your older child to help with the baby and be "Mommy and Daddy's big helper." When the new baby is napping, try to spend some special time alone with your older child.

Pets

The response of your friendly pet to the newborn can be similar to a sibling response—and just as unpredictable. Animals do get jealous and can hurt the newborn.

Never leave an infant and pet unsupervised.

"Babies are beautiful, wonderful, exciting,

enchanting, extraordinary little creatures—

who grow up into ordinary folk like us."

—Doris Dyson quoted in
What is a Baby? 1982
by Richard and Helen Exley

An Introduction to Understanding Your Infant

I have always felt that the first two months of a baby's life are like an extension of the nine months in the womb. They need total care and sustenance from you, but they don't seem to give much back in return. Occasionally, their eyes meet yours and a dreamy connection is made. It is not until two months, when not only do their eyes open widely at the sight of your face, but also they give you something wonderful—a smile!

What an honor! A baby's smile is the first social gesture that he/she will make in this world—and you are the first one to see it! This is the beginning of your relationship with your baby and it signals the end of the newborn period and the start of the infancy stages. Even if you have adopted an infant after the newborn period, the relationship begins with the first mutual smile.

Every month, your baby will grow at a rate faster than at any other time in his/her life, besides adolescence. Your baby will develop large muscle skills, fine motor skills, the beginnings of language and an increasing ability to socialize with the world.

You will soon learn that your baby is a unique combination of innate traits, genetic materials, environmental influences and something called "temperament." All of these characteristics combine to form a baby's personality—a reflection of who they are and how they will interact with the world and with those who share in their world.

Discovering the uniqueness of your baby and understanding their temperament will help you face any challenges that may arise during the first year of life. Since every baby is different from the start, what works for one baby and parent may not work for another.

You will, however, receive so much advice from so many sources that you may begin to feel unsure of yourself. Remember, no one knows your baby better than you do! Trust your instincts and enjoy the many wonderful experiences awaiting you and your baby!

Keep These Points in Mind

Your baby is a unique individual. Celebrate this uniqueness, but learn to work with your baby's temperament and personality.

Babies develop at different rates. Don't fall into the parent comparison trap! Even with siblings! Enjoy the differences.

Remember that advertisements are aimed at your insecurities. Be a good consumer. Carefully examine products and their claims before purchasing and read unbiased comparisons before making decisions.

Normal loving and stimulation is all that a baby requires for growth and development. Think basic and simplicity when selecting toys. Avoid electronic toys and "educational" products.

Savor this time with your infant. Remember this wise old saying: "The days are long, but the years are short."

"(Becoming a parent) is still the biggest gamble
in the world. It is the glorious life force.
It's huge, scary—it's an act of infinite optimism."

—Gilda Radner
(Comedienne)

Your Two Month Old

Congratulations! You have survived the hardest two months with your new baby. Although it may take a little bit longer to really get to know your new little wonder, most babies have already found their place in the family by two months of age.

Feeding and Nutrition

The main source of nutrition for your baby is still either breast milk or formula. Solid foods should not be given before four months of age. Early introduction of solid foods can cause problems for some infants because their digestive tracts are immature and are not ready to digest and absorb more complex foods. It is not true that cereal will make a baby sleep through the night.

Breastfeeding

By this time, you and your baby have established a good nursing relationship. You may notice a "let down" or feel an increased fullness in your breasts just as your baby is getting hungry.

Continue nursing on demand. Although most babies will need to nurse every three to four hours while awake, some babies may still require feedings every two to three hours at this age. During growth spurts, your baby may need to feed more frequently. At night, your baby may require at least one, and possibly two feedings, but if your baby is sleeping through the night, enjoy! Continue to take your prenatal vitamins and have some fluids while you are nursing.

Formula Feeding

Iron-fortified formula is recommended from birth to prevent anemia. Most babies will be taking six ounces of formula per feeding at this time (a few will be taking eight ounces without spitting up). The average baby will take between 16 and 24 ounces of formula a day.

No Microwaving

It is recommended that you refrain from heating formula or expressed breast milk in a microwave oven. Serious mouth burns have been caused by "hot spots" in microwaved liquids. It is safest to warm a bottle in a pan of heated water.

Vitamins

Most formula fed infants, drinking at least 17 oz. per day will get their daily vitamin requirement from formula. If you are breastfeeding, the Academy of Pediatrics recommends a vitamin supplement containing Vitamin D to prevent rickets in infancy, a bone softening disease caused by Vitamin D deficiency. However, most women if they get 10-15 minutes of natural sunlight 2-3 times per week will produce adequate levels of Vitamin D.

If you are breastfeeding and are in situations that limit the amount of sunlight that you take in through your skin, you may be at risk for Vitamin D deficiency, and therefore so may your infant. Living in urban areas or high latitudes, staying indoors most of the time, or covering most of your skin with clothing while outside are all Vitamin D deficiency risk factors. If you feel you may be at risk, then discuss with your doctor about the need for Vitamin supplements.

Infant vitamins usually come as a tri-vitamin containing Vitamins A, C and D or as a multivitamin which includes the B-complexes as well. Your pediatrician will help make the decision about the need for vitamins and which type might be best for your baby.

Sleeping

Although some babies sleep through the night by two months of age, most babies do not. Breast-fed babies will often require a nighttime feeding for the first several months since breast milk is digested more rapidly than formula.

Sleeping through the night ("settling") does not mean that you can put the baby down at 8 p.m. and wake him or her at 8 a.m. It does mean a five to six hour period of sleep, which will occur sometime between the hours of 11 p.m. and 7 a.m.

Sleep Position

Because of recent concerns that sleep position may be related to Sudden Infant Death Syndrome (SIDS), the American Academy of Pediatrics made the following recommendation:

Healthy infants should be positioned on their side or back when being put down for sleep.

For infants with certain medical conditions, your pediatrician or family practitioner may recommend another sleep position.

Siblings

Remember to allow free time for all caretakers to spend time playing with each individual child. Your older children also need your time and attention. A good time for attending to older siblings is while the baby is napping. Also, encourage siblings to become involved in the care of the new baby.

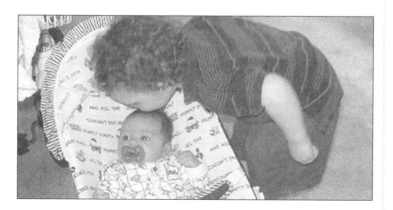

Pacifiers

Babies have a tremendous need to suck. It is their method of releasing tensions and it is a very important self-soothing behavior. Some babies will suck their fingers; others prefer a pacifier. If you choose to utilize a pacifier, use one which is constructed in one piece. Orthodontic nipples are preferred.

Pacifiers should never be hung around the baby's neck with ribbon, string, or any other type of material, as this presents a choking hazard.

Dressing

Dress your baby as you dress yourself—dress appropriately for the weather outdoors. Use common sense when weather is extremely cold or extremely hot.

Safety

DVD Chap 7

Important Safety Notes:

- Never put a rear-facing car seat on the front passenger side.

- Place infant seats away from table edges.

- Never leave your baby unattended on any elevated surface.

- Never drink hot beverages while holding your baby.

- Avoid jewelry on your baby.

Car Seats

Car seats should remain facing the rear until your baby weighs 20 pounds and is 12 months of age. A rear-facing infant car seat cannot be placed on the front passenger seat if that seat has an airbag installed. The safest place for children under the age of 12 years is in the back seat. Infant seats designed for home use should never be used as car seats.

Infant Seats

Babies should be securely strapped into infant seats and placed away from table edges. The safest place for a baby in an infant seat is on the floor.

Changing Tables

Never leave babies unattended on changing tables.

Burns

If you have not already installed smoke detectors in your home, do so now. Never smoke, drink or prepare hot beverages while holding the baby.

Avoid scalding

Lower the thermostat on the household water heater to 120° F to prevent burns from too-hot water.

Choking

Avoid putting jewelry on your baby. Especially necklaces or bracelets that are choking hazards. Children should never wear necklaces or bracelets to sleep.

Outdoors

It is best to keep your baby well-shaded. Avoid sunburns by using a PABA free sunscreen of SPF 15-30 on any areas exposed to the sun.

Development

DVD Chap 5,6

Babies are born with their own temperament and unique personalities. Every baby develops at his own pace. No one book on infant development will describe your child. I know it is difficult, but try not to compare your child with others! Your pediatrician or family practitioner will be following your infant's development with you at each visit.

Two-month-olds are learning to smile. It is truly a wonderful moment when your baby responds to you after all your hard work. As your baby is rewarded with smiles in return, smiling will occur more often.

A daily change of environment is also good for everyone. Take your baby out to explore the world.

Your baby will love mobiles and cradle gyms. Most babies love brightly colored objects, high-contrast black and white designs with primary colors, big round shapes (especially faces) and mirrors.

Your baby's hand becomes a new "toy" by about three months of age. Hands are loosening up and are less often held in a closed fist. Babies may stare at their hands for hours. Your baby can hold a rattle placed in the hand, but cannot yet reach for it.

You will notice increasing vocalization, with your baby making echoing sounds. Take time to cuddle and talk to your baby. By three months of age, your baby will turn in the direction of a sound. Babies love music and singing, as well as just "chatting."

By this age, babies have increasing neck strength, but remain wobbly until four months of age. It is not dangerous to practice standing if you have a baby who wants to be in that position. However, most babies will not be able to support their own weight on their legs at this point.

Because babies are now placed on their backs to sleep, some babies have developed a flattening of the backs of their heads. To help avoid this, it is recommended to place the baby on his or her tummy for short periods, or to keep the baby held upright in order to counter the time spent on the back of their heads.

The Next Doctor's Visit—Four Months

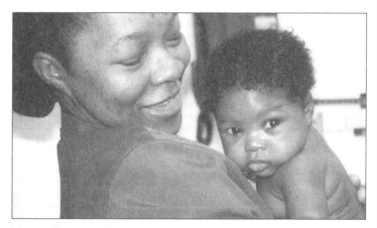

You will probably return to your pediatrician or family practitioner when your baby is four months. If you have any questions or concerns before your baby's next visit, do not hesitate to contact your pediatrician or family practitioner.

"He is also coming to sense that he makes

things happen in the world...When he turns his head,

the scene always changes. When he closes his eyes,

the world always grows dark. When he moves his arms,

he always feels the sensation from their movements...

In this way he is coming to appreciate that he

is an actor, an active agent in events."

–Dr. Daniel Stern
(speaking of a baby at four months)
Diary of a Baby, 1990

Your Four Month Old

Four-month-olds are the most delightful babies! They seem to be waking up to the world and wanting to take it all in. Everything delights them—especially their parents and siblings!

Feeding and Nutrition

Breast milk or formula continues to be your baby's main source of nutrition. While it is possible to start some solid foods at this point, there is no rush. It is okay to wait until the baby is six months old.

Breastfeeding
The time between nursing should increase feedings during the day and longer periods at night. A night feeding is not unusual for breast-fed babies at this age.

Formula Feeding

Most babies will take six to eight ounces at a feeding and, generally, take four to five bottles per day. The amount of formula the average formula-fed baby takes is 32 ounces per day. Most babies' iron supplies are used up between four and six months of age. That is why iron-fortified formula has been recommended since birth.

Juice

Your baby can have a small amount of juice (three to four ounces per day.) This is optional, however, and you do not need to start giving juice at this time if you do not wish to. Apple juice diluted with water is a good choice with which to begin. Citrus juices can cause diaper rash in some infants who are sensitive to them. Remember—this is a new food and should not be introduced at the same time as any other new food.

Solids

The American Academy of Pediatrics recommends beginning solid food between the ages of four and six months. Nutritionally, your baby does not need to eat solid foods until six months when his iron stores become depleted. It may take some time before your baby learns to eat from a spoon and swallow solid food.

Remember to introduce only one new food at a time. Allow three to four days between new foods to make certain your baby does not have a sensitivity or an allergic reaction. Signs of sensitivity to food include vomiting, diarrhea and gas. True allergy involves the immune system. Signs of allergy in infants include skin rashes, wheezing, vomiting and diarrhea. If this occurs, you should call your pediatrician or family practitioner to discuss it with him/her. It is a good idea to keep some children's diphenhydramine (Benadryl) in the house in case of an allergic reaction. If your child has a minor reaction to a particular food, wait one to three months and reintroduce the food. If she has the same reaction, this is likely more than a coincidence.

If your baby tolerates the new food, it can be combined with other foods that have already been introduced. For example, if you already have given rice cereal, you may add applesauce at the same meal.

Common Questions Regarding Starting Solid Food

"How do I know if my baby is ready?"
Eating solid food from a spoon is a new developmental task for your baby. Some babies are ready early and others are not. There is no reason to rush. Signs of readiness include good head control, interest in your food, and a shorter time between feedings.

If your baby is pushing the food out with his tongue, crying, or closing his lips, it is too early. Wait a few weeks and try again. When your child is developmentally ready, eating is an enjoyable experience for parent and child.

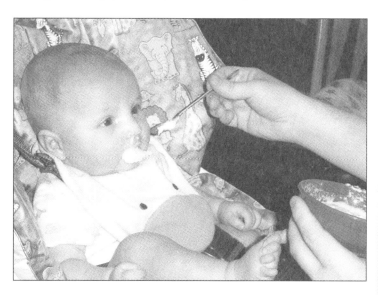

"In what order should solid food be introduced?"
I recommend cereals, yellow vegetables, green vegetables, fruits and finally meats. Some recent research has shown that children who start vegetables before fruits may like their veggies better when they are older. This may be because fruits are sweet and babies instinctively love sweet food.

"What should I start with?"
A single-grain iron-fortified cereal is a good choice. Most people begin with rice cereal because it is less allergenic. Squash and sweet potatoes are good first vegetable choices. After introducing cereal and vegetables separately, you can mix them for a nice meal.

"How should I mix the cereal?"
You can use breast milk, formula, or (for an older child) juice. Apple or orange juice mixed with iron fortified cereal is thought to increase iron absorption. Check the label for instructions for the first feedings. A thin consistency is better for beginners. Make the cereal thicker as your baby's tongue movement and swallowing becomes more coordinated.

"How much should the baby eat?"
This depends on the baby. Let the baby lead you. When she anticipates the next bite with an open mouth and a smile, she probably wants more. When she shuts her mouth and turns her head, she is letting you know she's finished. Resist the urge to force that last spoonful. Trust your child's ability to regulate her own growth. The average serving size of cereal is four tablespoons. Most children will eat between one half and one jar of fruit or vegetables. Respecting your child's appetite sets the stage for healthy eating behavior in the future.

"What time of day should the meal be?"
It is up to you. I suggest a morning meal. If your child has a reaction to a new food, it would be better to have it in the light of day.

"When should I start a second meal?"
When your baby takes the first meal well, you can begin a second meal. By eight to nine months of age, your baby should be eating three meals a day.

Drooling

By four months, most babies are drooling and putting their hands into their mouths. This does not necessarily mean the baby is teething, but it is probably an early phase in the teething process. If the baby's skin gets irritated from the drool, use a barrier ointment such as the brands A&D or Vaseline on the face before bed and place a cloth cotton diaper under the head.

Sleeping

You should continue to put your baby to sleep on his back (or side). If your baby is not already falling asleep on his own, you may want to begin teaching him to do so. Place him in the crib when he gets sleepy so that he learns to fall asleep there. This will help in the coming months, when he wakes up during the night (normal after six months of age) and is not hungry. He will then be able to settle himself down to sleep again on his own without you, the bottle or breast. Some babies may not be able to do this until after six months of age. It is normal for the vast majority of breast-fed babies to be nursed to sleep.

Safety

DVD Chap 10

Important Safety Notes

- Never leave your baby unattended on any elevated surface.

- Never drink hot beverages while holding your baby.

- Be alert for small objects that your baby can now put into his mouth.

- Avoid walkers.

Falls
Most four-month-olds can squiggle, squirm and roll right off a changing table or any other elevated surface. Many parents do not believe this until the baby falls! Never leave your child unattended on any surface, raised or not.

Burns
Make it a house rule—never smoke or drink hot beverages while holding the baby.

Choking
Avoid jewelry, small objects or clothing with buttons. The baby will be starting to put everything in her mouth at this age.

Walkers
Thirty to forty percent (30–40%) of children who use walkers have injuries ranging from pinched or trapped fingers to falls down the stairs to accidents in the kitchen. There is also some evidence that walkers interfere with normal walking by overdeveloping some muscle groups. The American Academy of Pediatrics discourages the use of walkers. Stationery exercisers, such as brands like Rollaround Exersaucer, are safe after six months of age.

Development

DVD Chap 8&9

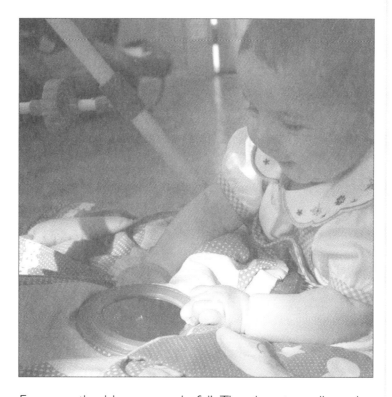

Four-month-olds are wonderful! They love to smile and laugh, especially at faces and bright colors. They can move their arms and legs at a rapid pace. They show pleasure when pulled to a sitting position.

When on their backs or in infant seats, they will reach for hanging objects. By five months, they will be able to bat at and maybe even get hold of an object. Good toys for babies this age include anything that hangs over the baby (be sure to avoid any objects with sharp edges or small pieces.) There are a number of companies that make links, which can be used to hang toys over the baby at varying heights. The best toys may turn out to be the baby's own hands, which he may study for hours. Next will be the feet and toes!

You will also notice that the baby is putting his hands together in the middle of the chest and moving them toward his mouth. If a rattle or toy is placed in the baby's hand, he will love exploring it (especially with his mouth!) Both hands and feet will be taken into the mouth by six months of age.

You will hear cooing and early babbling. This will include squeals of delight and sometimes screeches. Music is very important. Don't be afraid to sing to your baby (they are gentle critics!)

By five months, your baby should have good control of his head when in a sitting position. Most babies will not sit unassisted until six months. Your baby will be able to bear some weight on her legs by now, too. When placed on the stomach, she can lift her head and chest off the ground, and may even start rolling over soon. Be sure to include "tummy time" so she can practice these skills.

You may find that, for the first time since she was born, the baby can occupy herself and you can take a break. Don't be afraid to do this! You still remain the center of your baby's universe.

The Next Doctor's Visit—Six Months

You will probably return to your pediatrician or family practitioner when your baby is six months old. If you have any questions or concerns before your baby's next visit, do not hesitate to contact your pediatrician or family practitioner.

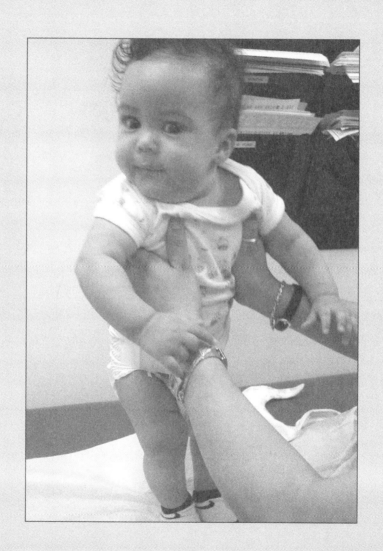

"Babies need social interactions with loving adults who talk with them, listen to their babbling, name objects for them, and give them opportunities to explore their own worlds."

—Sandra Scarr
(Developmental Psychologist)
Mother Care/Other Care, 1984

Your Six Month Old

Six-month-olds are ready to explore as they develop a sense of what they like and dislike as well as the beginnings of their own self. They respond, babble, start to move and are just fun to be with!

Feeding and Nutrition

Breastfeeding

The number of nursings per day varies with each baby. You may continue to feed on demand. At this point, use your judgment and instincts to tell you how frequently your baby needs to nurse. Most babies do not need night feedings after six months of age. Feedings at night are more for comfort now.

Formula Feeding

Iron-fortified formula has been recommended since birth because your baby's iron stores begin to run out between four and six months. Most babies will take three to four bottles per day (for a maximum of 32 ounces per day) between six and nine months. Over the next several months, your baby's diet will transition from predominantly liquid to predominantly solid foods.

Solids

If your child has not started solid food, you may begin now. Offer solid food first and follow your baby's lead. He will communicate when he has had enough. Be a good listener. Never force your child to eat. Respecting his appetite sets the stage for healthy eating behavior in the future.

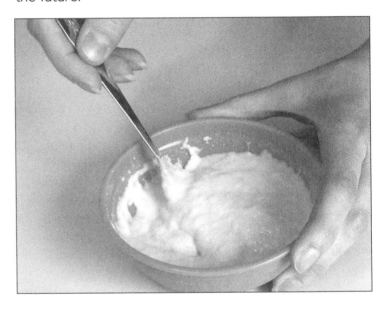

The introduction of solid food generally proceeds from cereals to yellow vegetables to green vegetables to fruits and finally to meats. If your baby is already tolerating cereals, vegetables, and fruits, you can continue by adding meat to her diet. Remember to introduce one new food at a time and wait three to four days before beginning another.

Single meats have more protein than the mixed dinners. Avoid mixed dinners until later in the year when he is also taking other protein sources. In the beginning, half of a small jar will be plenty. Lighter meats, such as chicken and turkey, are easiest to digest, followed by ham, veal, lamb, and then beef. Some babies may refuse the single ingredient meats. If you have smelled them, this will not be surprising. If this is the case with your child, try mixing the meat you are eating with broth and blending it.

By six to nine months of age, your child will advance to three meals per day depending on when you started solids. Breakfast is typically cereal mixed with fruit. Lunch can be yogurt (plain or mixed with a jar of baby fruit,) cottage cheese and fruit, or other pureed foods you prepare yourself. Dinners should include a protein source (such as meat) and a vegetable. Some parents prefer to offer the largest meal at midday.

Your baby will show interest in experimenting with finger foods once he develops a pincer grasp (placing the forefinger and thumb together). Good beginner finger foods include bananas and other soft fruits, soft cooked vegetables, Graham crackers or Cheerios. Even without teeth, a baby can gum foods to a pulp. Remember, eating is a developmental task. Some babies can handle Cheerios at six months, but others may find it difficult until eight or nine months. If your child has a particularly sensitive mouth, you may find he gags on textured foods. Do not be alarmed. As he gets older, his gag reflex will diminish.

Typical Servings:

Stage 1 or First Foods:
Fruits and vegetables = 1/2 jar to 1 jar

Strained foods = 1/3 to 1/2 jar

Junior foods = 1/3 to 1/2 jar

Strained or junior meats = 1/2 to 1 jar

Chunky foods = 1 jar

Dry cereals = 4 tablespoons

Feeding Tips

Don't offer baby food right from the jar unless your baby eats the whole jar at one time. The enzymes in the baby's saliva may make leftover baby food watery.

When feeding, place the spoon on the middle of the baby's tongue to avoid her reflex to push it out with the tongue.

Warm or Cool?

Most babies will accept foods at room temperature, but even young children prefer some foods cool and others warmed. Vegetables, meats and combination meals may taste better warm, while juices, fruits and desserts can be served cooled. Cereals can be mixed with liquids that are warm, cool or at room temperature.

To Safely Warm Baby Food:

- Use an electric or hot water feeding dish.

- Simmer (do not boil) water in a pan, then set a heat-resistant glass bowl containing the food in the heated water. If your baby will take the whole jar at a feeding, you may place the jar in the water.

- Microwave in a microwave-safe dish. Stir the food after heating and check the temperature with your finger in at least two places in the food. Never microwave meat sticks, which can explode.

Storing Baby Food Safely

Unopened jars of baby food and cereal should be stored in a cool, dry place. Avoid extremes of temperature and never freeze baby food.

Unopened jars of food can be safely stored for many months. Each jar has a date on the cap; use food before the date expires for best quality. If the jar lid has a safety button, make sure you hear and see it pop when you unscrew it.

Leftovers and Opened Jars
Throw away any food that has been heated and served. Don't return leftovers to the jar.

Once a jar has been opened (but not served,) the remaining food can be stored in the refrigerator for two to three days. After that time, unused food should be discarded.

"Orange Babies"
If you find that your child's skin becomes orange, it is most likely because she is eating too many orange vegetables. The pigment in carrots, squash, sweet potatoes, cantaloupe and peaches can turn your baby's skin orange. This is known as "carotenemia." It is not dangerous. Her skin will return to its normal color when she cuts down on these foods.

Foods to Avoid
Peanut butter, egg whites and shellfish are highly allergenic and should be avoided until after the first birthday. Egg yolks can be given at nine months.

Many children get diaper rash from citrus juices, therefore we recommend holding off on orange and grapefruit juice until your child is one-year-old.

Avoid any foods, which pose a choking risk such as nuts, popcorn, raisins, olives, raw carrot sticks, hot dogs, and prevent access to hard candy and gum as well.

Making Your Own Baby Food
Some people prefer to make their own baby food for economic or nutritional reason. To do this safely, please consult a book or reference on this topic.

Juices/Water
As your baby begins to eat solid foods, she will need extra water and/or juice to help her kidneys clear the extra protein in the diet. Add the extra fluids with meals. This is a good time to introduce a "sippy cup" at the same time. Juices do not have to be diluted. We recommend no more than four to six ounces of juice per day at this age.

Vitamins
A multivitamin preparation should be continued as per your pediatrician or family practitioner recommendations.

Fluoride
Fluoride strengthens developing teeth and helps prevent cavities from forming. Remember, even permanent teeth are forming during the early years. However too much fluoride can cause a discoloration of the teeth called fluorosis.

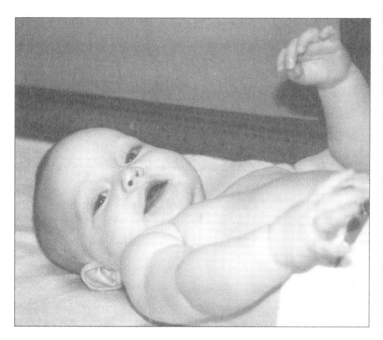

Discuss with your doctor if the water in yor area is fluoridated and if any supplementation with fluoride is necessary for your baby. When given in the correct dosage fluoride is not a health hazard and will not discolor teeth.

If your baby does receive fluoride be careful to avoid fluoridated bottled water or toothpaste that contains fluoride. Your baby might swallow the toothpaste during brushing. Your pediatrician or family practitioner will prescribe either a vitamin containing fluoride or fluoride drops.

Teething

The first teeth usually erupt between five and twelve months of age and are usually the two bottom incisors (the teeth in the middle.) There is great variability in the timing and sequence of tooth eruption.

When teething, your baby will want to mouth and bite everything in sight. You can provide him with cool, hard objects such as frozen bagels or teething rings. Avoid plastic rings filled with water as these may harbor bacteria. Some babies like to chew on a frozen wet washcloth (wet the cloth, twist it and place it in the freezer).

Acetaminophen (Tylenol) or ibuprofen (Advil or Motrin) can be used to control discomfort. Fever, up to 101° F, is common when teething. Other symptoms commonly associated with teething include runny noses and loose stools.

The two most important things you can do for your baby's teeth are cleaning them after feeding and to avoid putting the baby to sleep with a bottle filled with milk or juice. Putting the baby to bed with a milk or juice bottle can cause "baby-bottle caries" (a mouthful of rotting teeth) which can require extensive dental repair, even complete removal of teeth. Ideally, the teeth should be cleaned after the last bottle is finished. You can even do this after the baby has fallen into a deep sleep.

Tooth Care
Clean the teeth either in the morning or evening. You can do this with a washcloth during the baby's bath, using plain water and gently rubbing along the teeth. This can also be done with an infant toothbrush.

Sleeping

There are many different sleep methods and practices among different families and different cultures. If you decide that you want to sleep with your infant, you must understand that this is a long-term commitment. Co-sleeping must continue at least until 18–24 months of age because of the profound separation anxiety experienced by babies between nine and 15 months of age.

Co-sleeping is defined as a baby sleeping in close

proximity to a parent. This can be in the same bed or in a bassinet or crib near the bed. Many breastfeeding mothers prefer this arrangement because of the ease of night feedings. There is a body of research that supports the safety of infant co-sleeping and some researchers believe that co-sleeping has a healthy effect on the breathing and sleep patterns of newborns.

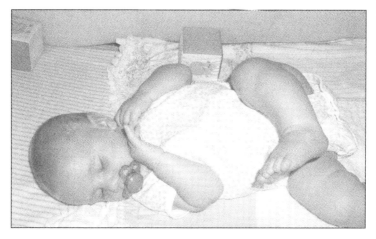

If you want your baby to sleep in her own crib and separate room, now is a good time to establish bedtime routines and prevent bad habits from developing.

Many experts on infant sleep stress the importance of teaching your child to soothe herself to sleep. They suggest that you let your child find a way to go to sleep without your active involvement. Finger sucking is a common method chosen by babies (some will suck pacifiers, but they are harder for an infant to find by themselves.)

During the second half of the first year, most babies sleep through the night. However, they also begin to have normal periods of waking during the night, as do adults. To go back to sleep, they must duplicate the conditions under which they went to sleep in the first place. If these conditions include you, then you will be getting up one to three times a night to rock, feed or hold your infant until sleep recurs.

A cuddly blanket or stuffed animal can become a "transitional" object, helping the baby make the transition away from you to sleep. The hardest part of this is letting your baby fuss or cry a bit when you lay him down. The temptation is to help the baby by rocking. This can backfire and leave you drained and exhausted if you have an infant who wakes more than once a night.

Other important points about sleep

Formula fed babies at this age do not require a feeding in the middle of the night. If they get one regularly after six months, they will become trained to be hungry at night and this makes the situation more difficult to reverse. Avoid feeding if at all possible.

Five to ten minutes of crying or fussing at this age is not harmful to the child but is painful for you. If crying increases, or goes on for longer than ten minutes, go in and offer comfort. Gently and gradually increase the time between going back into the room.

Each family situation is different and I offer these comments as guidelines only. Please discuss any problems you are having with your pediatrician or family practitioner.

Safety

DVD Chap 13

Important Safety Notes:

- Car seats should remain rear-facing.

- Be extra cautious of choking hazards.

- Never leave your baby unattended for even a second on any elevated surface.

Car Seats

Remember car seats must be rear-facing until the baby is 20 pounds and 12 months of age. Read individual manufacturer's instructions to ensure that your current seat can be used past the newborn period.

Choking and Poisoning

Because the six month old puts "everything" in her mouth, this age is high risk for both these accidents. In addition your baby can now pick things up with her fingers. So be extra cautious with any small objects, pills, or poisonous plants that could be within your baby's reach.

Falls

Babies can now roll and therefore can very easily fall off beds and changing tables. Always keep one hand on your baby (or change diapers on the floor!)

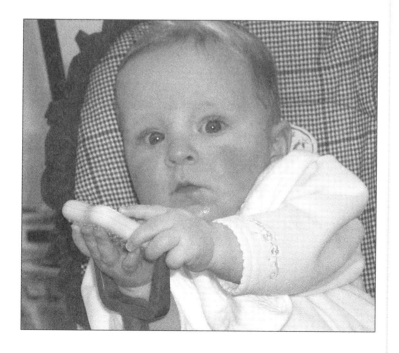

Development

DVD Chap 8&9

The six-month-old is starting to explore the world beyond his own body. Social activities over the next few months will include expressing likes and dislikes, stretching out the arms to be held, looking for a toy after it drops, patting a mirror image, keeping the lips tightly closed after having been fed enough, and trying to get attention with coughing or other sounds.

By six to eight months, most babies will have developed a fear of unfamiliar faces, known as "stranger anxiety" and may cry when parents or caretakers leave the room. This is commonly known as "separation anxiety." Both result from the child's realization that he is a separate being from his parents and can be separated from them.

Fine motor skills are developing rapidly. The baby will be able to reach out and pick up many objects, transferring them hand to hand. Objects will be explored by mouth. The baby should also be able to hold his own bottle (although many prefer not to.) Some may also begin to drink from a cup.

Babbling will be the first language, with strings of one syllable sounds and some combinations of syllables. You may notice that the baby has an increased response to his name, as well as some reaction to a strong "No!"

Most babies will sit unsupported by seven months of age and stand holding onto the crib rail or your hand. Rolling will increase from front to back and then back to front (but this is very variable from infant to infant.) A few babies will begin crawling at this stage.

The Next Doctor's Visit—Nine Months

You will probably return to your pediatrician or family practitioner when your baby is nine months old. If you have any questions or concerns before your baby's next visit, do not hesitate to contact your pediatrician or family practitioner.

"Parents who want a fresh point of view on
their furniture are advised to drop down on all
fours and accompany the nine or ten month old
on his rounds. It is probably many years since
you last studied the underside of a dining
room chair. The ten month old will study
this marvel with as much concentration
and reverence as a tourist in the Cathedral of Chartes."

—Selma Fraiberg
(Child Psychologist)
The Magic Years, 1959

Your Nine Month Old

Nine-month-olds are coming into their own as motor skills, language, response and self awareness are all developing rapidly. With the newfound abilities, you and your baby will enjoy more exploration and socialization!

Feeding and Nutrition

The majority of your baby's calories should come from solid food by now. At this age there is wide variation in what children are eating. Some children eat pureed foods only, while others have advanced to table food. Most children are somewhere in the middle. As your child's pincer grasp improves, allow her to feed herself. This can be messy, so spread plastic under the highchair or feed your child in an easy-to-clean area like the kitchen.

Breastfeeding

Babies who are breast-fed will now need three to four feedings per day. It is normal for many babies to nurse frequently during the day. Nursing remains an enjoyable and comforting experience.

If you are planning to wean your baby from the breast, do it gradually over a period of several weeks. You can replace one feeding at a time over a period of several days. This method will prevent problems for both of you. If you have any questions, feel free to discuss them with your pediatrician or family practitioner.

Formula Feeding

Most babies require only three bottles a day (24 ounces) at this age.

Introduction of Cow's Milk

Cow's milk is not recommended until one year. Early introduction of milk can cause anemia for two reasons. First, cow's milk is a low iron food. Continuing formula until one year guarantees your child an adequate iron supply while the baby is expanding her diet. Second, reactions to cow's milk proteins that may occur in the baby's immature intestine can contribute to anemia. The disadvantages of formula are the cost and the time involved in preparation. If this is a factor, let your pediatrician or family practitioner know.

Solids and Finger Foods

If you have not introduced meat into your baby's diet, do so now. If you are planning a vegetarian diet, alternative protein sources can be used. Consult your pediatrician or family practitioner for tips as well as a knowledgeable nutritionist.

You can begin using foods with more texture (Stage 3, junior meals, or table foods.) Combination meals may be used, but be aware that they are less nutritious than combining foods on your own. If you are using jarred foods, the baby should be taking one jar of meat or two combination dinners per day. The amount of fruit and vegetables will vary, but you should strive for the following in one day: one jar of meat, two servings of fruit and two servings of vegetables. A serving may be one half to one jar, depending on the baby.

If you are planning to advance to finger foods, offer soft cooked chicken, thin cold cuts, soft cooked fruits and vegetables, crackers, bread, and cheese. You can be as creative as you like as long as your baby can tolerate the texture and consistency of the foods. If your baby is "choking" on everything, go back to pureed foods for a while.

We recommend that you avoid feeding egg whites, shellfish, citrus products, honey from the jar or peanut butter until after the baby's first birthday.

Avoid Choking Foods
Do not give the baby nuts, popcorn, raisins, hard candies, raw vegetables, uncut grapes, hot dogs, and gum.

Salt, Sugar and Additives
Children are born with a taste for sweets but salt is an acquired taste. Remember, your job as a parent is to offer healthy food to your child and it is his job to eat it. There is no reason to give your child highly salted or sweetened foods at this age. Let him enjoy the natural taste of foods. It is worth the extra effort to prevent your child from developing health problems associated with the overuse of salt and sugar. Most baby foods, except fruit desserts, are prepared without added sugar or salt. However, some of the junior and toddler foods still contain a great deal of salt and sugar. Read labels carefully.

There is a lot of truth to the saying "you are what you eat." It could also be said that "you eat what you buy!" A little meal planning at the grocery store goes a long way toward helping you provide a healthy diet for your baby.

Juices and Water

As your baby decreases his breast-milk or formula consumption, it is important to increase his water and/or juice intake. But be aware that too much juice is not healthy for your baby. The high sugar content can decrease the baby's appetite for other foods. Try to limit juice servings to under eight to 12 ounces per day.

The Cup

Your baby will begin increasing the use of the cup at this point. You will need one with a lid and spout, since babies enjoy spilling as well as sipping!

Sleeping

Hopefully, you and your baby are sleeping through the night by now. However if you are breastfeeding it is normal for your baby to continue to feed during the night. You may have encountered "night awakenings." These are normal occurrences that happen for all of us during the sleep cycle. We are usually unaware of them and we turn over and go back to sleep. The baby may not be able to put himself back to sleep if the sleep conditions are not duplicated. If the problem is just beginning, enter the room quietly. Don't turn on the lights or talk to your baby. Comfort your baby (in the crib is best) and, hopefully, she will return to sleep. A common mistake is to feed or play with your baby, who will begin to enjoy this routine, but doesn't have to get up and work in the morning! If problems persist, discuss them with your pediatrician or family practitioner.

Safety

DVD Chap 16

Important Safety Notes:

- Install safety gates at all stair landings.

- Plug electric outlets with safety covers.

- Cut or tie shade and blind cords to keep out of your baby's reach.

- Toilet seat covers should be latched shut and bathroom doors kept closed.

- Latch cabinet doors in kitchen and bathroom.

- Post Poison Control number by your phone.

- Take a CPR course.

- Be careful with plastic bags (tie them into a knot before disposing).

- Keep swimming pools gated and locked. Never leave a baby unattended in or around the pool.

Falls

As your baby increases her mobility, you will find that the number of bumps or bruises on her body also increases. Try your best to create and maintain a safe environment. Install gates at stair landings. Never leave the baby on an elevated surface.

Electricity

Plug electric outlets with safety covers. Get electrical cords out of the way of the baby's mouth and reach.

Poisoning

Your baby can now move purposefully toward objects and grasp them. Putting them into the mouth is still the major mode of exploration. All potential poisons (medicines, vitamins, iron, cleaning products, alcohol, etc.) should be moved to high locations.

Place safety latches on cabinet doors. You can leave one kitchen cabinet unlatched and place safe plastic toys and containers or pots and pans in there for the baby to explore and play with.

I highly suggest you obtain the phone number for your local Poison Control Center and post it prominently by your phone or where you or a caretaker can quickly access it. If you believe your baby has ingested a poison, call the number immediately, even before you call your pediatrician or family practitioner. They will give you information on how to treat your baby. The American Academy of Pediatrics no longer recommends using syrup of ipecac to treat ingestions.

CPR

Check with your local American Red Cross Chapter for courses available in your area.

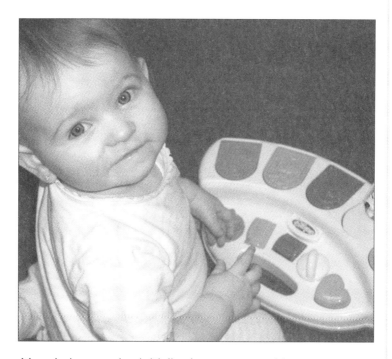

Development

DVD Chap 14&15

Your baby may be initially shy or wary with strangers. This is called "stranger anxiety" and may happen even with family members if they are infrequent visitors. This occurs because your baby can now distinguish between familiar and unfamiliar faces. Your baby definitely knows his parents.

Your child is also becoming aware that parents and caretakers are separate beings from himself. It is a scary time for a baby. He may cry even when you just walk out of the room. This is a good time to say "bye-bye" when you are really leaving the baby. Never try to sneak out. This way, the baby will not develop anxiety from not knowing what is really happening.

A helpful game is "peek-a-boo." You will notice that your baby loves this game now. It is no coincidence. The game helps relieve separation anxiety by practicing your disappearance. When your baby is older, he will

learn to pull down whatever is covering you with a shriek of delight. This game gives your baby a sense of control over the situation.

Separation for sleep may become a problem. You will notice more crying at this time. Develop a routine to help make the transition to sleep easier by including rituals such as reading a bedtime story or singing a song.

A "transitional object" is useful for sleep and stressful separations. This can be a cuddly toy or smooth blanket, which your child can use to ease the anxiety.

You can encourage use of this object by placing a favorite toy or blanket near you and your baby during feeding or cuddle times. He will begin to associate you with the object. Some children attach to transitional objects, some do not.

Enjoyment of social activities is increasing. Your baby will enjoy "reading" picture books, taking objects from you, and offering objects to you (it may not be until later on that the object is released to you!)

Fine motor skills are increasing as your baby begins to pick objects up with his thumb and forefinger, bang cubes together, and put objects into and take them out of containers.

Language improves, with increased babbling and combinations of syllables, new consonant sounds, and maybe even one word with meaning. Dada or Mama may become associated with Mom or Dad. Mothers: do not be offended if "Dada" is first. The hard "D" sound is easier to pronounce and does not indicate a preference of parent. The baby will respond to (but also frequently ignore) "no!"

Your baby should be sitting unsupported by eight months and may begin to stand, holding onto the furniture. Some babies may pull themselves up to a standing position.

Some babies will be crawling, some may not. A few babies will be "cruising" around the furniture or even walking alone over the next few months. The beginnings of walking varies considerably from baby to baby. If you have concerns, contact your family practitioner or pediatrician.

The Next Doctor's Visit—Twelve Months

You will probably return to your pediatrician or family practitioner when your baby is twelve months old. If you have any questions or concerns before your baby's next visit, do not hesitate to contact your family practitioner or pediatrician.

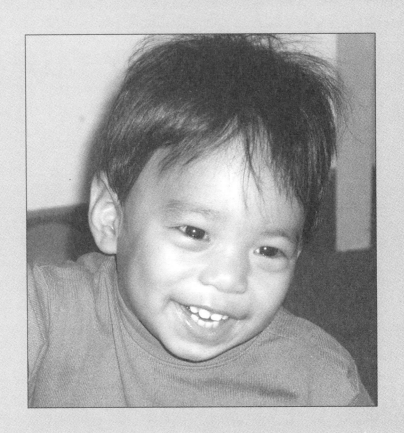

"The child supplies the power, but the
parents have to do the steering."

–Dr. Benjamin Spock
(Pediatrician and Author)
Dr. Spock's Baby and Child Care, 1985

Your Twelve Month Old

Happy First Birthday! Your baby is now a little person who is very mobile, determined and opinionated. The challenge becomes how to balance your child's desire to explore and enjoy his newfound freedom while keeping him safe from harm.

Feeding and Nutrition

Breastfeeding

The American Academy of Pediatrics recommends breast milk for the first year and beyond. When you decide to wean your baby is a very personal choice. Babies who are still nursing generally feed three times a day with some shorter feedings added for comfort.

Introducing Cow's Milk

Now is the time to change from formula to whole milk. Although there is still some debate amongst the experts of whole milk (3.5% fat) vs. low fat (1% or 2%) milk, your baby will probably do well either way. Discuss the choice with your doctor. If your child is drinking a standard cow's milk formula, feel free to just switch. If your child was sensitive to milk as an infant, you may want to go more slowly. Most children outgrow milk protein allergy. Replace one to two ounces of formula per day with whole milk. Observe for vomiting, diarrhea, skin rashes and blood in the stool. If your child is drinking soy or rice milk, check the label to be sure it is a calcium fortified product.

Some babies prefer milk to food. Too much milk can lead to iron deficiency anemia and should be avoided.

Cow's milk does not contain iron and it can cause small amounts of blood loss from the digestive tract. A large amount of milk also reduces your child's appetite for other foods. The American Academy of Pediatrics recommends no more than 16–24 ounces of milk per day. Your baby will receive enough calcium from this amount. Other sources of calcium include cheese, yogurt, tofu, soybeans, green leafy vegetables and calcium-supplemented products such as juices, some frozen yogurt, some cereals and waffles. Infant cereal is an excellent source of iron and should be continued as long as your baby will accept it.

Solid Foods
Most of your infant's solid food meals will be finger foods. Your baby should be encouraged to feed himself.

This can be messy but it will reduce struggles at mealtime. Spread newspaper or plastic beneath the high chair. Your baby will develop a real sense of achievement once self-feeding is mastered.

Introduce a beginner spoon with a wide, easy grip handle to help get your baby accustomed to the use of utensils. Practice with plain or vanilla yogurt, infant cereal and mashed potatoes. They don't stain! By 15 months, your child will start to get the hang of self-feeding with a spoon.

Decreasing Appetite

Most children experience a reduction in their appetite between 12 and 15 months. This is due to a normal decline in their growth rate. Trust your child's ability to regulate his own intake. It is your job to decide what is offered, and his job to decide how much he wants. The more you try to force your child to eat, the more he will resist. Most toddlers eat one good meal a day. If your child refuses a meal, he will be hungry for the next. This is normal toddler behavior. Allowing him to feed himself whenever possible is the best way to avoid battles. Resist the temptation to offer junk food in a desperate attempt to get your toddler to eat. They are very perceptive. He will quickly realize that if he holds out he can get what he wants! Look at every meal and snack as an opportunity to offer healthy food.

Have realistic expectations of how much your toddler will eat. In general, toddler portion sizes are approximately one quarter of an adult portion.

> **Typical toddler servings:**
>
> - Rice or pasta – 1/4 cup cooked
>
> - Bread – 1/4 slice
>
> - Vegetables – 1 tablespoon per year of age
>
> - Fruit – 1/2 piece or 1/4 cup
>
> - Milk – 1/2 cup
>
> - Cheese – 1/2 oz.
>
> - Yogurt – 1/3 cup
>
> - Protein – 1 oz.

The Cup Versus the Bottle

You should begin weaning your baby from the bottle over the next few months. How easy this will be depends on how attached she is to her bottle. Offer water and juice in a cup. Change milk bottles to the cup over a period of weeks. The morning or evening bottle is generally the last to go. Express delight when your child drinks from the cup, even if half of it winds up on the floor!

Vitamins and Fluoride

Continue to give your child multi-vitamins and/or fluoride if prescribed by your pediatrician or family practitioner.

Teeth

Most babies will have four to eight teeth by now. Remember to continue daily tooth care and to avoid putting the baby to bed with a juice or milk bottle.

Shoes

If you haven't bought a pair of shoes by now, this is a good time to do so. There is a great deal of discussion regarding infant shoes. The controversy centers around whether high-topped shoes are better than low shoes and whether shoes should be made of leather or if sneakers are okay. In fact, it doesn't make a bit of difference as long as the shoe or sneaker fits well and your baby can walk in it. We advise purchasing any pair of shoes or sneakers that protects the feet while allowing the development of the foot muscles. Your baby's foot should be measured to ensure proper fit.

Safety

DVD Chap 19

Important Safety Notes:

- Use safety latches, locks, and plug covers to child-proof your home.

- Place gates at the top and bottom of all stairs.

- Remove or cover cabinets and tables with sharp edges.

Child-Proofing the House

With increased mobility, you must increase your "child-proofing" of your baby's environment. If your baby is walking, she can now reach taller heights. Latches, locks and plug covers are very important. Walking also brings bumps and bruises. Watch for sharp edges on cabinets and tables. Remember to place gates at the top and bottom of stairs.

Poisoning

Make sure all potential poisons, cleaning fluids, insecticides and prescription or OTC medicines are kept in locked cabinets. I highly suggest you obtain the phone number for your local Poison Control Center and post it prominently by your phone or where you or a caretaker can quickly access it.

Development

DVD Chap 17&18

Most one-year-olds have overcome their stranger anxiety and have emerged as social butterflies. They want to jabber to everyone and make their audience laugh. They want to play games with you. They may kiss on request, imitate you and delight in offering you food. In general, they want to explore everything in their environment.

They are also struggling for independence at this time. They are torn between staying close to home base and walking or cruising as far as they can go. This is a source of anxiety for a while. Frequently, your one-year-old will go a distance away and then return to home base for a touch or hug of reassurance—then off she goes again!

Real anger may make its first appearance, when your baby encounters frustration. It is unusual to have a full-blown tantrum at this age, but you will definitely know when your baby is angry. Since you must protect your curious explorer from danger, you will be forced to show disapproval. Frequently, a stern "no!" will do. This may bring a great deal of crying, but it is an important learning experience for both of you.

Not all children will be walking at one year. Some children begin walking at 15 or 18 months. If your baby is "walking" on hands and feet like a bear, or standing and holding on to furniture and cruising around, this is normal. Although it is difficult, try to avoid comparisons with other children.

If your baby is walking now, you may see anger and frustration emerge when you attempt to restrain him or her for diaper changes and other necessary daily activities. Distraction becomes the name of the game. I recommend you place a toy on the changing table. You may even need to learn to diaper your child standing up!

Watch out—the major milestone after walking is climbing!

Fine motor skills are increasing your baby's dexterity and he or she can now pick up even the smallest piece of lint on the rug. After mastering this pincer grasp, your baby can release these objects to you. The practice of this skill,

known as "casting," is the feature of a favorite game in which the baby releases objects from the high chair to the floor for you to retrieve! This also relates to the baby's experimentation with objects and how they move. This is not an act of defiance and should not be discouraged or punished. This is an important developmental stage and you do need to allow it to take its course.

Language is increasing, with the baby understanding simple phrases and questions. Most infants will begin using two or three words besides "Mama" and "Dada." By 13 months of age, most babies can make their desires known through a combination of words and gestures.

By twelve months, your infant has become a very special person. At this age, your baby should make good eye contact, smile, make noises and "try to speak" with others. If at any time over the next several months you are concerned about your baby's language development or social interaction, please discuss this with your pediatrician or family practitioner.

Over the next two to three months, you will notice that the baby wants to empty everything and this includes every garbage container in the house. Through this activity, they learn the concepts of "contained" and "container." It may be annoying at times, but if you remove the unsafe items and allow this period of exploration, you will be helping your baby learn important lessons.

Good toys for the one-year-old include sturdy baskets and push toys. Be sure that these toys can support the baby's weight in order to avoid injuries. Soon after walking is mastered, your baby will love pull toys, especially those that make noises. Toys that your baby can hammer on are also enjoyable.

The most difficult task you, as parents, will face over the next few months is balancing the baby's need to explore with your need to protect him and keep him (and your possessions) safe from harm. To reduce the amount of "no" in your baby's life, remove valuables and child-proof the house as best as you can. Use distraction as much as possible by replacing one object or activity with another. When you do have to say "no," do it firmly and consistently. Eventually, your baby will get the message.

How you handle your baby in this first stage of discipline will have an impact on later stages. It is difficult to be firm with your baby, but you must help the baby learn to live with limits and to deal with frustration.

The Next Doctor's Visit—Fifteen Months

As always, if you are concerned about any area of your child's development or behavior please discuss it with your pediatrician or family practitioner.

Child Care and Special Situations

Working Outside the Home

Many mothers today are returning to work as early as six weeks after delivery. The decision of whether or not to return to work and when to return to work are personal ones and the decision should be made by your family. Try not to be influenced by relatives or the media.

Children do well if they are cared for by people who care, whether it is one-to-one with a nanny or family member or a quality day care center. The childcare arrangement you ultimately select will depend on the baby, your finances and your work responsibilities. Only you can make this decision, but if you have concerns or questions, it is a good idea to discuss your decision with your pediatrician or family practitioner.

Adoption

The information in this book applies to any baby adopted during the first year of life. However, there may be special situations that require more information and attention. It's important to understand the special bonding and attachment that occurs between adopted infants and parents.

If this has been an international adoption there will be many important medical and developmental concerns that should be addressed by your pediatrician, family practitioner or a specialist in international adoptions. Usually a developmental pediatrician will become involved to help you and your infant "catch up" on developmental milestones. (*See the Resource and Reference section.*)

Multiple Births   Although most of the information in this booklet will apply to any number of babies, if you have twins, triplets or quadruplets you may need some additional information and help. There are many good books and resources both locally and nationally, including online Web sites that can provide both support and additional information. Most helpful are local organizations that put mothers of multiples in touch with one another. (*See the Resource and Reference section.*)

Special Situations   Premature infants and infants born with special needs may also require additional information and support. The advice on routine care contained within this booklet will still apply to most babies, however, we encourage you to discuss any concerns either with your family practitioner, pediatrician or the specialist caring for your baby. (*See the Resource and Reference section.*)

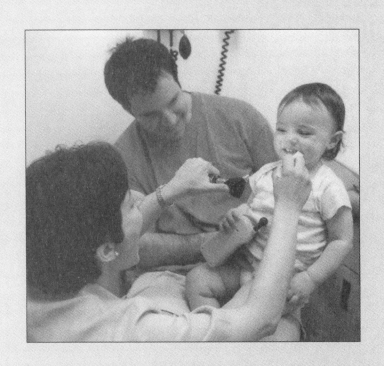

Your Baby's Pediatric Care

Scheduled Doctor Visits

The schedule of visits to your family practitioner or pediatrician may vary, but the following guidelines suggested by the American Academy of Pediatrics are most widely used.

During the first week of life, especially if you leave the hospital at 48 hours or less, the doctor may ask you to bring the baby in to make sure there is no significant jaundice, or to check the baby's weight if that has been a concern.

Two Weeks

Most important at this visit is the baby's weight. The baby's weight should be close to or greater than birth weight at this visit. At this and all the baby's future visits, your physician will measure the baby's height, weight and head circumference. He/she will plot these measurements on standardized growth charts so that he/she can track the baby's growth. Also at this visit, feeding will be reviewed and any further questions you might have will be addressed and answered.

Two Months to Two Years

The American Academy of Pediatrics suggested schedule of well-child visits is: 2, 4, 6, 9, 12, 15, 18, and 24 months.

At each visit your pediatrician or family practitioner will look for expected developmental milestones. Feeding will be reviewed and safety issues, which pertain to babies at each particular age, will be reviewed.

A series of vaccinations will be given to your baby during the first two years of life. The schedule is frequently adjusted and may vary from state to state. Your pediatrician or family practitioner will guide you and provide you with a schedule. A test for tuberculosis is also given at some time during the first two years of life. In some states, a blood test to screen for anemia and lead exposure is also performed.

Recommended Vaccines:

DTaP – combined diphtheria, acellular pertussis
and tetanus

Hemophilus B (HiB) vaccine

Hepatitis B

Influenza vaccine

IPV – polio vaccine

MMR – measles, mumps and rubella

Pneumococcal vaccine

Varivax – Chicken pox vaccine

Immunizations

Why do we immunize?
We immunize our children to protect them from very
serious and often life-threatening diseases. Vaccines
provide immunity by introducing the disease in a weak-
ened or killed form into the body. The body's immune
system then produces antibodies to the disease and
this provides immunity. The only other way to gain
immunity is to actually have the disease.

Are there risks to my baby from vaccines?
Overall, the risk to your baby's health from these
vaccines is very small. The most frequent side effects
are fevers or rashes, or swelling at the site of the injection. Some vaccines, however, carry more risk then
others for serious side effects. Your pediatrician or family
practitioner will discuss these risks as well as the benefits
of the vaccines before your child receives them. You
will also receive written information about the vaccines.
Please read this information carefully and ask any
questions before your child receives the vaccines. It is
the overwhelming conclusion of both the American
Academy of Pediatrics as well as the Centers for Disease

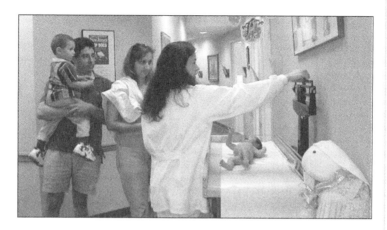

Control (CDC) that the benefits to immunization outweigh the very small risks involved. However, you must feel comfortable making this decision.

Is there a relationship between the MMR (Measles, Mumps, and Rubella) vaccine and ASD (Autistic Spectrum Disorders?)
In recent years, this question has been raised in many public forums. Scientists generally agree that most cases of ASD result from events that occur before a baby is born or shortly after birth. However, the symptoms typically emerge in the second year of life—about the same time the MMR is administered. Because of this, there has been concern that there is a relationship between the MMR vaccine and ASD.

In response to these concerns, the Centers for Disease Control and Prevention (CDC) and the National Institutes of Health (NIH) asked the Institute of Medicine (IOM) to establish an independent expert committee to review all hypotheses regarding this question. (The full report can be read on www.CDC.gov/NIP also see www.AAP.org.)

The committee concluded that the vast majority of cases of autism cannot be caused by MMR vaccine and that the recent increasing trends in autistic diagnoses cannot be explained by the rate of immunization with MMR in this country. Research and review continues into the safety of all vaccines and the establishment of an independent scientific committee of this purpose is an important step forward in vaccine safety.

Is thimerosal used as a preservative?
Thimerosal is a preservative that was originally used in some vaccines to stop the growth of bacteria. There is no evidence that thimerosal containing vaccines cause any harm in children, and no link has been found between thimerosal and ASD (Autistic Spectrum Disorders). Yet some researchers raised concerns about exposing small infants to mercury in the thimerosal. Therefore the FDA and the pharmaceutical companies decided to remove thimerosal as a preservative from all routine childhood vaccines. It still exists in some preparations of the influenza vaccine, however it is not thought to pose any risk for the infant receiving the vaccine. Since influenza vaccine is now recommended, the supplies of preservative free vaccine will probably be increased over the next few years.

Do I have a choice?
All parents have a choice. You should be provided with information on the risks and benefits of each vaccine so you can make an educated decision. It is the recommendation of the American Academy of Pediatrics that all children be as fully immunized as possible in order to protect our children and society from these contagious and dangerous diseases.

Is immunization required for school entrance?
Every state has its own requirements for vaccination. Some states are very strict about vaccinations and school attendance. This is especially true for pertussis and measles vaccines, and some children have been barred from school or day care until the vaccine was given.

If you decide not to immunize your child at all or only to immunize with certain vaccines, it will be your responsibility to deal with the local school board. Your pediatrician or family practitioner may or may not get involved unless there has been a medical contraindication to receiving the vaccine.

Does my child have to get the shots at the doctor's office?
Most family practitioners and pediatricians provide the vaccine as a service to their patients. You may be able to obtain these vaccines at your town's local health department or clinic. At most clinics, the vaccine is administered free of charge for eligible patients. If your child does not receive his vaccinations at your family physician's office, please let them know the date of the vaccination, so that they can keep your child's records up-to-date.

What are the diseases vaccines immunize against?
Diphtheria is a severe infection of the nasal and breathing passages. A toxin is released into the body and can cause other areas (such as the heart and neurologic system) to become affected. Ten percent of infected patients die from this illness. Vaccination against diphtheria has been so successful in this country that there are fewer than five cases each year in the United States.

Tetanus (also known as lockjaw) can result from contaminated wounds or punctures. A toxin is released into the blood, which causes stiff neck and difficulty swallowing, followed, by painful muscle spasms. It is almost always fatal.

Pertussis (also known as whooping cough) begins with a mild cough and cold but then progresses to severe paroxysms of coughing ("the whoop") often followed by vomiting. Breathing becomes difficult because of the coughing spasms.

Even after the whooping stage, the patient can be ill for many weeks with cough. Other complications include convulsions, pneumonia, and neurologic damage or death. The disease is very severe if it occurs during the first year of life. For infants less than eight months, the death rate is one percent (1%) of infected children. There are still 3,000 to 4,000 cases reported in the United States each year, and many more mild cases occur in adults each year. There is no cure for pertussis and care is usually supportive in the hospital.

Polio results from a virus. Most cases occur without any symptoms or present as a very mild flu-like illness. Permanent paralysis can result.

Measles is a viral illness. Patients have a cough, cold symptoms, red eyes and a distinctive red rash that looks as if a bucket of red dots was poured over them.

Most cases are uncomplicated but pneumonia is a common complication. Less common is encephalitis (or inflammation of the brain) in one out of 2,000 cases. Survivors often have permanent brain damage. Death occurs in one out of 3,000 cases in the United States.

Mumps is a viral disease that causes swelling of the salivary glands. Encephalitis is a complication of mumps. Orchitis (infection of the testicles) occurs in post-pubescent adolescents and adults. This can lead to sterility.

Rubella is also known as **German Measles.** This viral infection produces very little illness in healthy children and adults. It involves a rash, some lymph node swelling and fever.

We immunize children to protect infants from congenital rubella. This occurs when a woman who is pregnant gets rubella. The disease is devastating to her unborn child: deafness, eye abnormalities, heart defects and neurologic problems including mental retardation can result.

Hemophilus Influenza (HIB) is caused by a bacterium, not by a viral flu. It is a very common cause of infection in infants and children. The most serious infections caused by this bacterium are epiglottitis (swelling of the epiglottis or upper airway, which can rapidly become fatal) and meningitis. Although meningitis can be treated with antibiotics, complications such as deafness, brain damage, and death can still occur.

Chicken Pox (Varicella.) The majority of cases of chicken pox are uncomplicated. The child is uncomfortable for a week with itching, and sometimes pain and fever. Some cases develop complications, a few of which can be life-threatening. Before the vaccine was used, every year, between 50 and 100 people died from complications of chicken pox, half of whom were children. The most common complications in otherwise healthy children are skin infections—some of which can be very severe and even produce toxic shock syndrome—and pneumonia. Adolescents and adults can get the most severe cases of chicken pox with a higher complication rate. Less serious complications such as the potential scarring of chicken pox lesions are also a concern to many parents.

The varicella vaccine - Varivax - is a protection against chicken pox, but it does have some drawbacks. Natural chicken pox gives a person life-long and complete immunity from the disease. The vaccine does not guarantee 100% immunity. In clinical trials, the vaccine was effective 70–90% of the time. If a child who has had the vaccine does get chicken pox, however, it will be a milder form of the disease.

Protection from the vaccine may not last forever. Protection is known to last for 20 years, and researchers continue to follow and study this issue to determine if a booster will be needed.

Pneumococcus. Pneumococcal bacteria causes many infections in infants and children. The most serious of these infections are pneumonia and meningitis. Pneumococcus is the leading cause of bacterial meningitis in the United States at this time.

Hepatitis B was added to the list of diseases children should be immunized against by the American Academy of Pediatrics in 1992. Hepatitis B is a virus, that attacks the liver. Even though most illnesses are over within a few weeks, a percentage of patients go on to develop a chronic form of the illness, and this puts them at greater risk to develop liver cancer.

Hepatitis B can be acquired through exposure to blood or blood products, from sexual contact, and from mothers to infants at the time of birth. Most mothers are screened today while they are pregnant so that the doctor knows which mothers are carriers of the disease, and which infants need special treatment at birth. In rare cases, Hepatitis B can be acquired through close contact within families, from person to person through contact between open skin lesions, and possibly through saliva to mucous membranes (inside the mouth.)

Even though the highest risk period for infection is during adolescence and young adulthood, immunization of all infants is the goal. The advantages to immunizing infants are that they are immunized while they are within the healthcare system, and the dosage required (and therefore the related costs) are less. If an infant should contract Hepatitis B, he or she is more likely to develop the chronic form of the illness, so early vaccination is advantageous. The disadvantage is that researchers are not certain how long the vaccine protection will last, and there is a chance that your child may need a booster during adolescence or young adulthood.

Influenza. Although we commonly refer to a variety of viruses as the flu, the "true flu" is caused by the influenza viruses. These are very contagious and can spread rapidly through families, schools and offices. The symptoms are very specific and for older children and adults include high fever (usually lasting 4 - 6 days), sore aching muscles, generalized weakness, and headache, pain behind the eyeballs, a sore throat and hacking cough. More serious complications include pneumonia, encephalitis (inflammation of brain tissue) and serious secondary infections with bacteria. It is the overwhelming bacterial infections and respiratory complications that can be most deadly for young infants and are responsible for most of the hospitalizations. Although the majority of patients, including most infants and children, will recover fully, some patients will become seriously ill and require hospitalization.

Influenza can be a deadly disease for young infants and because of an increase in the deaths of healthy infants and children from influenza, the American Academy of Pediatrics is now recommending routine annual vaccination of all infants 6 months of age to 24 months of age. This will require two shots if the infant is receiving this immunization for the first time. It is also recommended that household contacts of children under 2 years of age also be vaccinated.

When to Call Your Doctor's Emegency Line:

You are the best judge of your baby's health. If, at any time, your child does not "seem right" to you, call your pediatrician or family practitioner. Learn to trust your instincts. Apart from that, you should call your doctor's emergency line if:

- A baby under three months of age has a temperature of 100.5° F or greater (taken rectally) or an older child has a rectal temperature greater than 105° F.

- "Projectile" vomiting (vomiting which seems to go across the room) occurs or repeated forceful vomiting especially if the vomitus contains blood or green bile.

- If your baby is bleeding heavily from a cut or wound.

- If your baby's stools contain more than a small amount of blood.

- If your baby is acting very irritable and lethargic or inconsolable (with decreased or no periods of alertness, no sucking or no eye contact.)

- Listlessness is present—the baby does not seem to interact with anyone while awake.

- Your baby is breathing very rapidly, you hear wheezing noises or continuous coughing is present.

- Croup (a barking sound made when your child coughs) especially in a small infant or if croup symptoms are unresponsive to steam or cool air.

- Stridor (a harsh noise made by an infant or child on inspiration.)

**When to Call
911 or the
Rescue Squad**

There are some problems when it is best to call 911 before calling your pediatrician or family practitioner's office. Make sure the phone number is posted near every phone in the house.

- Severe difficulty breathing, especially with blue coloring or after choking.

- Serious injury (especially with massive bleeding, obvious broken bones or severe head trauma with loss of consciousness.)

- Electrical shock or burn.

- Allergic reaction (especially with difficulty breathing, airway swelling or wheezing or any of the above with hives.)

- Near drowning.

- Unconsciousness or an infant or child that can not be easily awakened.

**When to Call
Poison Control**

Call any time an infant ingests a potentially poisonous substance or plant. If severe breathing difficulties or any of the above severe reactions are present, however, call 911 first.

REMEMBER TO CALL **POISON CONTROL** FIRST BEFORE CALLING YOUR PEDIATRICIAN OR FAMILY PRACTITIONER'S OFFICE AFTER AN INGESTION. Post your local poison control number near every phone in your house.

Common Medical Problems

This section is not meant to be an all inclusive listing of medical problems that occur in infancy. These are just some common problems and what you need to know. Whenever you need help with a sick infant your pediatrician, family practitioner and their office staff will be there to help guide you.

Taking the Temperature

The only really accurate measurement of temperature in the infant is by rectal method. Purchase a digital thermometer. To insert the thermometer, lubricate the tip and then place it into the rectum (about 1/4 to 1/2 inch deep.) Pinch the cheeks of the buttocks together to hold the thermometer in place. Any temperature over 100.5° F is considered a fever. **(In infants three months of age or less, if the temperature is greater than 100.5° F, call your pediatrician or family practitioner.)**

Avoid the use of temperature strips on the forehead, as these are inaccurate.

Avoid mercury thermometers because the mercury is toxic if swallowed.

Also avoid ear thermometers, which do not work well with infants.

Giving Medication

Typically, medication is given as either 1/4, 1/2 or 1 teaspoonful. Instead of estimating these measurements with an ordinary kitchen spoon, ask your pharmacist for a special medicine spoon or syringe.

Some infant medications (such as Tylenol, Advil and Motrin) come with their own droppers. These droppers should be used only with their respective medications.

Some medications should not be given with food or drink because this will interfere with absorption. You may find that if you have to force your young one to take the medicine he may gag. If this is the case, it is better to give the drug on an empty stomach.

Other medications should be given with food. If special instructions are needed, you will receive these with your child's prescription.

Important Medicine Notes:

- Since the concentration of medicines is not equal in drops and elixirs, never use one dosage with the other.

- An ordinary teaspoon does not equal a dropper.

Colds

Should the baby develop a simple runny or congested nose without fever, you can begin treatment with salt water nose drops (1/2 tsp. salt added to eight ounces of warm water) or salt water nasal spray (Nasal, Ocean). If you block the mouth with a nipple and the nose is stuffed, the baby has difficulty feeding and breathing at the same time. Place two to three drops or one spray in each nostril. If the mucous is visible at the tip of the nostril, use a bulb syringe to remove the mucous. Bulb syringes are also known as nasal aspirators and may be labeled "ear syringe." This will help your baby feed better if done right before meals. Don't overdo the use of the bulb syringe, however, since it can irritate a baby's nose. A cold water vaporizer will help to keep the room moist and the secretions loose.

Avoid giving any cold remedies (even those marketed for infants) to infants under six months of age before contacting your pediatrician or family practitioner.

If possible, it is best to avoid decongestants which can make the baby irritable, increase the heart rate and raise the baby's blood pressure. Also avoid antihistamines. These dry secretions and make it more difficult for the baby to get rid of them.

Seemingly innocent cold remedies can be harmful to an infant. Cases of seizures and heart failure from rapid heart rates have been reported. Antibiotics serve no purpose in the treatment of the common cold and should not be expected. The cold symptoms usually bother the family much more than they do the baby.

Constipation

If no stool is passed for more than four days, if the stools are hard and ball-shaped, or if the baby appears to be in pain when passing the stool, this may represent constipation. If there is blood on the diaper or in the stool, please notify your family practitioner or pediatrician so he/she can make sure it is simply local bleeding from passing a hard, formed stool.

After a four day period with no stool, I recommend that you insert 1/4 of an infant glycerin suppository into the rectum. This usually will produce immediate results. Follow this treatment by beginning to give the baby a mixture of one ounce of prune juice or pear juice to one ounce of water each day until a regular bowel pattern is attained.

Avoid the regular use of suppositories, baby enemas, rectal stimulation, or home remedies.

If constipation is accompanied by vomiting or other signs of illness are present in the baby, call your family practitioner or pediatrician immediately.

Diarrhea

In the first two months of life, diarrhea can develop without fever. Diarrhea stools are watery and may be foul smelling. An increase in frequency and amount of stool may be noted. Notify your pediatrician or family practitioner if diarrhea develops in a baby three months of age or younger.

Current recommendations are to allow a baby to feed through uncomplicated diarrhea. This means that if the baby is not vomiting and is not showing signs of dehydration, you can continue nursing the baby or giving your baby his regular formula.

If you are breastfeeding, continue nursing throughout the bout of diarrhea. If you are formula feeding, you may want to supplement with oral rehydration solutions (such as Pedialyte or Infalyte) if you cannot keep up with the stool losses. Your doctor will advise you if this is necessary.

If cow-milk based formulas containing lactose seem to make the diarrhea worse, you can temporarily start feeding the baby a soy-based formula (such as Isomil or ProSobee) or lactose-free formula (such as Lactofree.) Let the baby drink as much as he wants as often as he wants. You can maintain your baby on this formula for at least one week before going back to the baby's regular formula. You can continue solid food in an older infant (who is not vomiting) but try mild foods first such as banana and applesauce. Avoid other fruits and vegetables. Rice is usually a good choice as well. For older infants, salty crackers can be given.

Dehydration

When stool losses are not replaced by oral fluid intake, dehydration results. The signs of dehydration include a dry, sticky mouth, absence of tears, decreased urine output and a poor appearance overall. If this occurs, notify your pediatrician or family practitioner immediately.

Diaper Rash

If a rash is developing, change the baby's diaper frequently and immediately after soiling. Avoid occlusive diaper covers, especially at night (you can make the diaper "breathe" more easily by snipping the elastic leg bands around rubber pants or by cutting slits in the plastic covering of disposable diapers). Apply barrier cream liberally with each diaper change. These protect the skin by sealing out humidity and irritating factors that may be present in urine or stool. These also reduce friction.

You don't have to remove all of the previously applied ointment with each diaper change. Superficial cleansing followed by another application of ointment is sufficient. If diaper rash persists more than a few days, a yeast infection may have developed. Try adding an anti-fungal ointment such as the brand Lotrimen (sold over the counter as Athlete's Foot Cream) with each diaper change.

Ear Pain

Although it may be difficult to tell in a very young infant if they are experiencing ear pain, there are some clues. If the baby cries whenever placed down to sleep or laid down flat on a changing table, or if an older infant bats at their ear with a hand, or if the baby seems unusually fussy. This is especially true if the baby has signs of a cold or has a fever. If you suspect your baby may have an ear infection, call your physician's office to have the baby seen.

Fever

Fever is your baby's normal response to infection and is often the very first sign that an illness is starting. It is also a common cause of anxiety in parents and a frequent reason for calling the doctor's office.

Fever

> When should you call your family practitioner or pediatrician about a fever? –
>
> - If your baby is less than three months and has a temperature greater than 100.5° F, you should call your doctor immediately.
> - If your older infant or toddler has a temperature greater than 105° F.
> - If your baby has a fever and is very lethargic and does not improve after getting acetaminophen or ibuprofen.
> - If your baby does not make eye contact, respond verbally or smile.
> - If your baby is having difficulty breathing.
> - If a fever is accompanied by a rash, deep coughing or wheezing, severe vomiting, or in an older toddler or child, a severe sore throat, a stiff neck, headache, severe abdominal pain, or pain on urination.

Infants (older than 3 months) and toddlers typically have temperatures between 102° F-104° F. Fever can accompany a simple viral infection or indicate a bacterial infection such as in the inner ear, bladder, throat, or chest. In rare cases it can mean that the child has a blood infection or brain infection such as meningitis. It's important to remember that fever in and of itself is not dangerous. It is true that children between six months and six years can experience a convulsion with fever, but this only occurs in five percent of children. As frightening as the convulsion is, it is usually very short and causes no long- term damage to a child's brain. Of course, if this occurs you should call the rescue squad or take your child to be seen immediately to rule out any other problems.

The height of the fever is not as important as how your baby looks, especially after an initial treatment with acetaminophen or ibuprofen. One half hour after the medicine or a lukewarm bath, the baby should look a bit brighter. If your infant can nurse or drink some liquids, make eye contact, or maybe even smile at a familiar face, it's more likely to be a simple infection. But if your baby is very lethargic, avoids eye contact, has no moments of playfulness or interest in other people or toys, then the illness may be something more serious.

We treat fevers in infants to make them more comfortable. If your baby has a temperature of 101° F and is somewhat playful, you may not need to do anything at all. The treatment for fever is using a medication such as acetaminophen (Tylenol) or ibuprofen (Advil or Motrin) and following the directions for your baby's weight and age. Be careful not to use a teaspoon when a dropper is indicated. The older child syrups and suspensions are not as concentrated as infant drops.

Another method is to give your baby a lukewarm (not ice cold) bath. You don't have to immerse the infant in water, rather lightly rub water over the body to help evaporate the heat. It is best to do this 30 minutes after giving acetaminophen or ibuprofen to avoid chilling.

Drinking lots of cold liquids will also help bring down the body temperature. Increasing the amount of fluids is also necessary in babies with fever because they can become dehydrated more quickly.

Remember to avoid alcohol baths or rubs (babies can have convulsions from alcohol toxicity absorbed through the skin.) Dress your baby in light cotton underwear and pajamas to prevent the temperature from rising higher. Avoid layering of clothes or blankets, high room temperatures, or hot outside temperatures. Avoid aspirin or any product that contains salicylates (Pepto-Bismol) to avoid Reyes' Syndrome, a potentially deadly illness.

Fevers that accompany uncomplicated viral illnesses such as colds and sore throats usually last three to four days. If your baby has a fever that lasts longer than three days it is wise to call your pediatrician or family practitioner and have your baby evaluated. The younger the baby, the more important it is to call your pediatrician's office or to have the baby examined.

Thrush	If you notice that the baby's tongue or sides of the mouth are white all of the time and you cannot wipe off the coating, this may be a yeast infection. Your pediatrician or family practitioner will treat this by prescribing an anti-yeast medication.

Sticky Eyes	Often a baby's tear ducts are not completely open. Because of this, the eyes will have some crusting, particularly in the mornings. Take a warm washcloth and remove the crust in the morning or whenever it seems to be building up. If pus develops in the eyes, it will appear more moist and gooey than the crust. This maymean that a common eye infection (conjunctivitis) is present. This can be treated with an antibiotic ointment prescribed by your baby's doctor. This infection does not cause impairment of vision and is not dangerous.
	In some babies, the tear ducts do not completely open for several months. Excessive tearing may be observed when the duct is blocked. If this is the case, you may have to use the antibiotic ointment periodically until the tear ducts remain open permanently. Daily massage of the inner corner of the eye (near the nose) is helpful if a blocked tear duct is noted.

Vomiting	All babies spit up at different times, some more than others, but true vomiting will be much more forceful. If a small infant is vomiting, you need to call your doctor's office for advice. In an older infant you can manage this at home by the use of an oral rehydration solution (such as Pedialyte.) Give small sips (less than an ounce at a time) frequently rather than a large amount of liquid that will surely be vomited right back. If vomiting lasts longer than 24 hours and if it does not seem to slow down after the first 12 hours, please notify your physician's office.

BOOKS

General Information

Baby and Child Care by Dr. Benjamin Spock. Steven Parker, M.D. Pocket Books, 1998.
This classic has been updated recently, but some feel the tone is condescending. Good as a reference.

Caring For Your Baby and Young Child: Birth to Age 5 by Steven P. Shelov, M.D., F.A.A.P. The American Academy of Pediatrics, Bantam Double Day Dell Publishing, 1998.
A complete guide to the early years.

American Academy of Pediatrics Guide to Your Child's Symptoms by Donald Schiff, M.D. Villard Books, 1997.

Your Baby's First Year by Steven P. Shelov, M.D., M.S., F.A.A.P. (Editor and Chief) The American Academy of Pediatrics, Bantam Books, 1998.
Excellent reference—what the Academy wants you to know.

Parenting by Anne Krueger. Editors: Parenting Magazine. Ballantine Publishing, 1999.
A guide to your baby's first year of life. Easy to read, well organized and written. Excellent reference.

The Parents Soup—A to Z Guide to Your New Baby by Kate Hanley. Contemporary Books, 1998.
The companion to the online parentsoup.com. A compilation of advice from parents with supervision from pediatricians.

Breastfeeding

The Womanly Art of Breastfeeding by La Leche League International, 1997.
Now in its sixth revised edition, the La Leche League International classic title is expanded to include important references and additional resources for the breastfeeding mother.

The Complete Book of Breastfeeding by Marvin S. Eiger, M.D. and Sally Wendkos Olds. Workman Publishing Company, 1999.
Co-authored by pediatrician and La Leche League International (LLLI) Medical Associate Marvin Eiger and medical writer and member of LLLI Sally Wendkos Olds, the third edition of this book thoroughly explains and explores all aspects of breastfeeding. There are also chapters about the role of fathers, exercise, diet, beauty and nutrition, as well as information about nursing multiples, preemies and other special situations.

The Nursing Mother's Companion by Kathleen Higgins, RN. Howard, Common Press, 1995.
Well respected source of breastfeeding information.

The Nursing Mother's Guide to Weaning by Kathleen Huggins and Linda Ziedrich. Howard Common Press, 1994.
Many breastfeeding mothers express concerns about weaning when their babies are just a few weeks old. This book explores all aspects of weaning starting with historical aspects and ending with weaning a child over three and life after weaning. Offers practical and helpful advice that respects the needs of both mother and child.

Nursing Mother, Working Mother by Gale Pryor. Howard Common Press, 1997.
Mothers who have decided to combine breastfeeding with working will find this an immensely helpful and reassuring book. The author includes practical information about planning for and returning to employment, clear concise tips on breastfeeding, pumping, storing and transporting milk and possible alternatives to full time employment such as job sharing, working from the home and staying home full-time. The book suggests numerous ways mothers can build and maintain closeness with their babies in spite of separation.

Feeding

Child of Mine: Feeding with Love and Good Sense by Ellyn Satter. Bull Pub. Co., third edition, 2000.

American Academy of Pediatrics Guide to Your Child's Nutrition by William H. Dietz and Loraine Stern, editors. Villard Books, 1999.

Sleeping and Crying

PLEASE NOTE: Some publications may have been published before the American Academy of Pediatrics made recommendations on sleep position and may still suggest placing the baby to sleep on his/her stomach. The American Academy of Pediatrics does not recommend this position unless advised by your pediatrician or family practitioner.

Guide to Your Child's Sleep by George J. Cohen, editor. The American Academy of Pediatrics, Villard Books, 1999.
A new book, which hopes to sort out some of the conflicting advice parents receive.

Healthy Sleep Habits/Happy Child by Marc Weissbluth. Fawcett Books, 1999.
A popular book that reviews common problems in establishing good sleep habits.

Mothers

The Girlfriends Guide to Surviving the First Year of Motherhood by Vicki Iovine. Perigee Books, 1997.
A funny book filled with practical advice by those who have been there. Add a little edge and humor and it's a good book when you feel all alone.

I Wish Someone Had Told Me—A Realistic Guide to Early Motherhood by Nina Barrett. Academy Chicago Publishers, 1997.
Explodes the common myths and ideals about early motherhood. Enjoyable, reassuring and funny.

Fathers

The Daddy Guide: Real Life Advice and Tips from Over 250 Dads— Other Experts by Kevin Nelson. Contemporary Books, 1998.
Another good source for dads, including sections on insurance, saving for college.

The New Father—A Dad's Guide to the First Year by Armin A. Brott. Abbeville Press, 1997.
A great book for new dads. Funny, well written, excellent sections on temperament. I enjoyed reading it and I'm not a father.

Parenting Multiples

This Isn't What I Expected—Overcoming Postpartum Depression by Karen R. Kleinman, MSW. Bantam Books, 1994.
A thorough description of the emotional mood disorders that can occur after birth. Well written.

Overcoming Postpartum Depression and Anxiety by Linda Sebastian. Addicus Books, 1998.
Written by a psychiatric nurse with 25 years experience, it mixes anecdotes with good information.

Special Needs Section

Raising Adopted Children: Practical Reassuring Advice for Every Adoptive Parent by Lois Ruskai Melina. Perennial, 1998.

Having Twins by Elizabeth Noble. Houghton Mifflin Co., 1991.

Twins, Pregnancy, Birth and the First Year of Life by Connie Agnew M.D. Harper Perennial, 1997.

Caring for Your Premature Baby—A Complete Resource for Parents by Alan H. Klein M.D. Harper Perennial, 1998.

Babies with Down's Syndrome—A New Parents' Guide by Karen Stray Gundersen. Woodbine House, 1995.
Good reference with lots of numbers and Web sites. Reviews of common products.

VIDEOS

Safety

Could You Save Your Baby's Life? The CPR Review for Infants and Children. American Heart Association approved. Northstar Entertainment, 1999.

Breastfeeding

Follow Me Mum: The Key to Successful Breastfeeding (Glover R). From Australia, but worth the hunt. Best video on latch on and positioning I've seen to date. Reblact@iinet.net.au

Breastfeeding: A Mother's Guide presents Dr. William Sears discussing the basics of breastfeeding. The video demonstrates proper techniques, how to avoid discomfort, and outlines products available for the breastfeeding mother. The video is available from La Leche League International, PO Box 1209, Franklin Park, IL, 60131 Phone: 1-302-525-3243.

Sleep/Crying

The Happiest Baby on the Block by Harvey Karp M.D. Simple and well demonstrated technique for soothing babies. (Amazon.com or www.thehappiestbaby.com)

Your Baby Can Sleep—The Practical, Proven Method for Solving Your Baby's Sleep Problems. Child Secure, Amazon.com. The clear, simple, effective methods for helping your baby sleep in the first year of life.

NATIONAL ONLINE RESOURCES

For your convenience many of these links can be accessed from **www.simplyparenting.com.**

General Information

www.AAP.org
The American Academy of Pediatrics Web site. The official place with advice and information about every topic in pediatrics. Many of their books and videos are available on this site.

www.generalpediatrics.com
A website created by a general pediatrician at the University of Iowa which provides a search engine and links to topics on all areas of pediatrics.

www.tnpc.com
The National Parenting Center
(800) 753-6667
Reviews of the finest products and services for children and their parents.

www.parentsplace.com
A bit commercial but the popular **iVillage** site with information and advice for new parents.

www.parentsoup.com
Lots of tips and an opportunity to connect with other parents through a variety of chat rooms and online communities.

Breastfeeding

www.lalecheleague.org
La Leche League International
(800) LALECHE

www.medela.com
Information and products from the MEDELA company.

www.everythingmom.com
Lactation Resource Center Web Store.

www.breastfeedingonline.com
Information from our experienced Lactation Consultant.

Child Safety

www.aapcc.org
American Association of Poison Control Centers
(800) 222-1222
How to locate your local poison control number.

www.iafcs.org
International Association for Child Safety
(888) 677-IACS
Promoting safety awareness and injury prevention for children.

www.safekids.org
National Safe Kids Campaign
(800) 441-1888
National non-profit organization dedicated to the prevention of unintentional childhood injury.

www.perfectlysafe.com
(800) 837-5437
Child safety products for every room in your house—well organized catalog of safety items.

www.saferchild.org
Safer Child, Inc.
General child care information and links to other helpful sites.

Child Passenger Safety

www.preventinjury.org/specneeds.asp
Automotive Safety Program
National leader and expert in transportation of children with special health care needs.

www.nhtsa.dot.gov
National Highway Traffic Safety Administration
(888) DASH2DOT
Information on child passenger safety and car seat inspections.

www.carseat.org
Safety Belt Safe USA
(800) 745-SAFE
National, non-profit organization dedicated to child passenger safety.

Medical

www.Kidshealth.org
Wonderful site! The Nemours Foundation. Non-Profit dedicated to children's health. Non-commercial. Well written articles. Easy to use search engine.

www.vaccines.ashastd.org
CDC National Immunization Information Hotline and Homepage (American Social Health Association) with FAQ's about immunizations.
(800) 232-2522

www.ndss.org
National Down Syndrome Society

www.sidsalliance.org
Sudden Infant Death Syndrome (SIDS) Alliance
(800) 221-7437

www.sbaa.org
Spina Bifida Association of America
(800) 621-3141

Mothers

Caesarian/Support Education and Concern
(508) 877-8266
Information on Caesarian childbirth, Caesarian prevention, and vaginal birth after Caesarian.

www.depressionafterdelivery.com
(800) 944-4PPD

www.postpartum.net
Postpartum Support International
(805) 967-7636

www.mothersandmore.org
Support for women who interrupted careers to stay home with children.

Fathers

www.fathers.com
National Center for Fathering

**Special
Parenting
Situations**

www.mostonline.org
Mothers of Super Twins (M.O.S.T.)
Support network for families of triplets or more.

www.nomotc.org
**National Organization of Mothers of Twins Clubs
(NOMOTC)**
Support group for parents of twins and higher order multiple birth.

naic.acf.hhs.gov (no www.)
National Adoption Information Clearinghouse
Federally-funded one-stop resources for information on
all aspects of child adoptions.

www.parentswithoutpartners.org
Organization devoted to the interests of single parents
and their children.

www.2moms2dads.com
Offers information and support for gay and lesbian parents.

Please visit our Web site for articles
on parenting and your child's health
as well as other books and DVDs in our series.

www.simplyparenting.com

AVAILABLE NOW

Understanding Your Toddler

COMING SOON

Understanding Your Preschool Child

Guide to Common Illness in Children